Telepathy

Telepathy

How to Use
Your Power of ESP

Tom Pearson

Astrolog Publishing House

Cover Design: Na'ama Yaffe

© Astrolog Publishing House Ltd. 2005

ISBN 965-494-207-0

P. O. Box 1123, Hod Hasharon 45111, Israel
Tel: 972-9-7412044
Fax: 972-9-7442714

Published by
Astrolog Publishing House 2005

LIMIT OF LIABILITY

Extrasensory phenomena

What are "extrasensory phenomena" and "extrasensory abilities"? Are these abilities and senses obvious and perceivable like sight, hearing, and the other senses, senses that are at the disposal of most human beings, or are they perhaps unique phenomena that are granted to a privileged few? Are they "genuine" phenomena that can be subjected to research and scientific study, or are they "superstitions" employed by man in order to escape from irksome everyday reality? Is the belief in natural abilities advancing and constituting an additional step toward the New Age and the technologies of the new millennium, or is it a primitive belief that curtails human progress?

These questions, and many others, inspired many scientists to try to understand the nature of extrasensory phenomena.

While in certain cultures, people with extrasensory abilities were highly esteemed, used their abilities for the benefit (or destruction) of other people, and enjoyed the general support of the culture in which they lived, other cultures considered involvement of any kind in the extrasensory to be dangerous, "dark," and a kind of witchcraft that contradicted religion and sometimes normative "common sense." (Every era has its particular norms of "common sense.") In the Middle Ages, when the

7

involvement in the extrasensory actually flourished and alchemists investigated it in depth, people who were suspected of engaging in this type of activity were severely tortured, excommunicated, or burned at the stake. Abilities that we are more amenable to accepting and trying to comprehend today were thought to derive from contact with "Satan" or "demons." Mind-reading, telepathy, telekinesis (the influence of thought on objects), future prediction and so on had to be conducted clandestinely for fear of the church authorities and extreme social reactions.

However, despite all the attempts to quash them, those actions and abilities have not only survived to this day, but are blooming and flourishing. Having said that, it is not unusual to meet people for whom any hint of extrasensory activity sparks fierce opposition or trepidation. In the past, as in the present, there were people who felt that there was more to the world than what we can perceive with our five basic senses, and, with great courage, and sometimes under a torrent of withering social or scientific criticism, decided to go with their truth to the bitter end and investigate the extrasensory world. Their efforts were not in vain, since today these fields are being investigated scientifically, and the greatest "enemy" of understanding the world beyond the senses, namely science, is beginning to remove the barriers and the protective walls and relate seriously and scientifically to the possibility of the existence of these phenomena. This is an attempt to gain a scientific understanding of how they occur and to comprehend the way the universe works.

What are 'extrasensory phenomena'

Clairvoyance, Remote Viewing – The meaning of the word *clairvoyance* is "seeing clearly." This is the ability to see through the third eye, to see symbols, scenes, names and so on via the extrasensory sense of sight. Various parapsychologists call the person who has clairvoyance a *visionary*.

Clairsentience – This means "feeling clearly," extrasensory feeling. It is a person's ability to sense messages or information, as well as the feelings of other people who are either far away from him or near to him. Various parapsychologists call the person who has clairsentience a *feeler*.

Clairaudience – This means "hearing clearly." A person with this ability can hear verbal or sound messages without the interference of his own passive thinking. This ability is also called *audio*.

Clairagustine – This means "tasting clearly." It is the ability to sense a certain taste with the mouth and tongue without any contact with the food or beverage, and by means of this the person receives a message that is linked to this taste. "Smelling clearly" is also generally included in this category – this is the ability to smell something that does not necessarily exist independently in the inhaled air, but rather comes in order to transmit a message that is linked to smell.

Psychometry – This word means "measuring the soul." A person with this extrasensory ability can read the energetic frequencies that a certain object emits, and this enables him to read the personality of the object or the events it has gone through.

Medical intuition – This is the ability to pick up the energy surrounding the person's energetic bodies and describe how the person's thoughts are realized in substance.

Telepathy – This is the ability to receive messages and information transmitted without words or body language. The extrasensory phenomena include a certain degree of telepathy, and people with extrasensory abilities generally develop telepathic abilities to some or other extent.

Aura-reading – Aura-reading is generally an ability that is added to one or more of the above-mentioned extra-sensory abilities, in accordance with the person's reinforced extrasensory sense (sight, feeling, etc.). Some people sense the aura by moving their hands over it or with an inner feeling; others see the shape of the aura and its colors around the person with their eyes open; still others see them with their "third eye," with their eyes closed. Some people receive information about the state of the aura intuitively, without seeing or feeling. Aura-reading is often an ability that is included in medical intuition or is added to it, or can be developed into useful medical intuition.

Receiving intuitive messages – This is inner knowledge of a certain message, event, or information, without seeing, hearing or feeling. This is a profound knowledge that can be considered as a "prophecy" when it reaches very high levels.

Channeling and medium – This is making contact with other dimensions or entities, and transmitting messages from them via the person who is channeling or the medium.

Radiesthesia – This is the use of a pendulum or a dowsing rod for a broad range of purposes, such as finding mines, locating lost people, receiving Yes/No answers, and so on.

Telekinesis – This is the ability to influence matter with the power of thought, such as bending teaspoons, lifting objects, stopping clocks, and so on, without physical contact.

Telepathy

The word *telepathy* originates from the Greek terms "tele" – distance, and "pathe" – event or feeling. The term *telepathy* was coined in 1882 by the French researcher, Frederic Mayers, the founder of the "Society for Parapsychological Research" (SPR).

Telepathy is one of the most common extrasensory modes of channeling. It is very easy to develop, and most people can discern its presence in their everyday lives. Furthermore, it has been extensively investigated by scientists, and today there is hardly any scientific dissent regarding its existence.

Telepathy is a channeling phenomenon between two brains. It includes the transmitting of information such as thoughts, ideas, feelings, and mental pictures. While in so-called "advanced" societies telepathy is considered to be a "sixth sense," a unique supernatural ability that is the gift of people with extraordinary extrasensory ability, older cultures, such as the Aborigines in Australia, see it as a natural ability belonging to the whole of mankind. As we will see in the chapter on supernatural abilities in animals, animals are also gifted with powerful telepathic abilities.

The research interest in telepathy began with the development of mesmerism and the interest in magnetism. The champions of magnetism discovered that they could sometimes transmit instructions or thoughts to their patients. Psychologists and psychiatrists quickly began to identify phenomena of this type in their patients. Freud discerned telepathic activities so often that he eventually had to relate to them in his writings. He defined telepathy as an ancient, primitive ability that had gotten lost during the course of evolution, but could still emerge under certain conditions. Karl Jung related to it as an important phenomenon, while the psychologist and philosopher William James was extremely enthusiastic about telepathy and encouraged its study.

In 1884, the "Society for Parapsychological Research" (SPR) was founded in Europe, and subsequently the American Society for Parapsy-chological Research (ASPR) was founded in 1885. Telepathy was the first extrasensory phenomenon to be investigated scientifically by these societies. The first telepathic tests were simple. The "transmitting" subject had to transmit a certain taste, two-digit number or visual picture from one side of the room to the "receiving" subject sitting on the other side of the room.

The interest in telepathy increased at the beginning of World War I, when many people who had lost close relatives turned to spiritualism (of which telepathy was thought to be a part) in order to attempt to make contact with their dead loved ones. Telepathy in Britain and the United States at the time became so popular that it engendered a party game. During that period, scientific and amateur research on telepathy began to flourish.

The findings of this research revealed that telepathy generally occurs spontaneously in certain cases of crises. When a friend or relative was injured or wounded, the person sensed telepathically that something had happened to him, and could sense that he was threatened by danger or experience a bad feeling. The telepathic feeling could occur in different ways – as a feeling that "something bad" had happened, in dreams, in mental pictures, in visions, in fantasies, in clear inner knowledge, and sometimes even by hearing or by words that pop into the receiver's thoughts. Frequently, the information that reaches the receiver causes him to alter his actions or plans, or simply to contact the person about whose welfare he is concerned. Moreover, many cases of telepathy between people and animals were discovered.

Another finding that emerged from the studies was that telepathy has a significant link with the emotional state of both the receiver and the transmitter of the message. The studies showed that most of the people with telepathic ability were women. One of the hypotheses regarding this finding was that women tend to be more in touch with their emotions and to listen more closely to their inner feelings. Having said that, it is possible that if these studies were performed today, the results concerning this particular issue would be different. Another interesting finding revealed that telepathy is very common in the elderly and geriatric age groups. The researchers' hypothesis states that the deterioration in the other senses may sharpen telepathic ability or lead to a better ability to listen to telepathic messages. The researchers discovered that in many cases, some kind of biological changes occur in the transmitter and the receiver of telepathic messages: changes occur in the transmitter's blood volume, while changes in the receiver's brainwaves occur in order to match the transmitter's brainwaves. Certain drugs, such as caffeine, are detrimental to the ability to transmit and receive telepathically.

Prof. J. B. Rhine was one of the researchers who promoted the study of the extrasensory in the most significant way. He established a research laboratory for studying extrasensory perception (ESP) at Duke University in North Carolina in the USA and conducted an in-depth study of the phenomenon of telepathy.

The main problem facing Prof. Rhine was finding the tools with which to examine and measure the extrasensory phenomena he was studying so that he could show findings that were as scientific and unequivocal as possible. Rhine reached the conclusion that accepted symbols, such as numbers from 1 to 9, are not suitable for examining telepathic abilities, since biases and prejudices were liable to cause most people to choose a certain number such as 7 more frequently than a less "popular" number such as 8. Together with Dr. Zener, another researcher in the field, Prof. Rhine developed the Zener cards, which have been used to this day for examining telepathic abilities. The Zener cards include five types of cards, each of which has a different shape on it – a circle, a star, three parallel wavy lines, a cross and a square. He chose these signs because they do not evoke any emotional or symbolic associations in most people. There are 25 cards in the pack, five of each kind. The subject must stare at the cards that are placed face down, and guess which of the five forms will appear when the card is turned over. In principle, the person will guess five cards out of the 25 correctly, on average. When the number of guesses exceeds five or is lower than five over a length of time, this attests to the fact that it is not random guessing, but rather the ability to guess more or less than the average. Levels of guessing that exceed the average attest to an extraordinary ability – the ability to see what is hidden.

Telepathy

After checking the efficacy of the cards, Rhine began a series of tests with the help of students who volunteered for the task. Initially, Rhine examined the subjects' abilities while they stared at the inverted cards. Then he began to ask them to answer without seeing the cards. The subject sat at one end of the room with a screen concealing the cards that Rhine turned over. Rhine soon found a group of subjects whose results were higher than average. One of the subjects, Pierce, astonished Rhine with his results. Pierce could guess about 10 out of the 25 cards – that is, a 40% level of accuracy (as opposed to the average level of accuracy of 20%).

Zener *cards*.

When he was so inclined, Pierce was able to guess only two out of the 25 cards – in other words, a lower than average result. Pierce's unique ability was reflected in the fact that before each test he was able to guess the number of cards Rhine decided that he would guess in that particular test. Even more amazing was his ability to guess the cards in a pack without them being spread out face down on the table in front of him. Pierce succeeded in making a list of the 25 cards and guessing eight of them correctly – far above the reasonable average. After this success, Rhine decided to make his experiments even more sophisticated. He began to increase the distance between himself and the subject. He and Pierce synchronized their watches and began to perform the test with Rhine initially in another room, and later on, in another building. At a certain moment, which had been agreed upon beforehand, Rhine would begin to turn the cards over, and Pierce, who was in a nearby building, began to write down the signs. Even in the distance telepathy experiment, Pierce's guesses were about 40% accurate.

In 1934, Rhine published a book based on the results of his tests. The book was not welcomed with open arms by the scientific community. It is possible that if Rhine had not made his name as a "serious" scientist prior to publishing the book, it would have received very harsh reactions.

In response to the publication of the book, Prof. Bernard Riess decided to repeat Rhine's experiments with the aim of refuting them as unscientific. Riess found himself changing from an opponent to a fervent supporter after a young girl who had participated in his tests succeeded in attaining an astonishing level of 70% correct answers! Once he had witnessed the phenomenon of telepathy with his own two eyes, Riess also began to investigate it. Prof. s was also one of the first researchers to examine the phenomenon scientifically. In his laboratory, he tested a person by the name of Shackleton, who claimed that he had supernatural powers.Shackleton was extraordinarily gifted – he could guess, with great accuracy, the sign on the card that would be revealed *after* the card revealed by the examiner.

After conducting his extensive research, Rhine reached the conclusion that it was not possible to make a sweeping separation in definition between telepathic abilities, clairvoyance, or precognitive clairvoyance – foresight or prediction. He concluded that telepathy and clairvoyance are the same extrasensory abilities that manifest themselves in different ways. In addition, he reached the conclusion that telepathy is not affected by distances or obstacles between the transmitter and the receiver.

A telepathic experiment that was conducted in 1971 after the launch of Apollo 14 proved that distance is not an obstacle to telepathic transmission and reception. The experiment was not authorized by NASA, and was not publicized until after the Apollo 14 mission was completed. The astronaut, Edgar Mitchell, conducted the experiment together with four "receivers" on earth, about 250,000 kilometers below the transmitter – Mitchell himself, who was in the spacecraft. Mitchell performed 200 sequences; guessing 40 of them would be a very reasonable average. Two of the receivers guessed 51 sequences accurately. The success of the experiment went way beyond Mitchell's expectations.

The numerous telepathic tests that were performed during the 1930s proved the existence of unexplained extrasensory phenomena to the scientific community, as well as to the general public, as well as the need for research on the subject. Over time, test means and methods improved in order to ensure that there would be no biases in the tests. Machines for shuffling the cards were invented, as were electric machines that linked examiner with subject and prevented eye contact or body language that could affect the results, and even machines that changed the place of the cards and projected the signs onto a screen by random choice of the order of the cards.

Among the general conclusions reached by the researchers, we will mention the four that are still considered valid after thousands of studies on the topic were conducted:

1. In tests of the Zener card type, there were people who could consistently achieve significantly higher or lower than average results, as they decided, throughout long sets of tests.

2. The ability to consistently achieve higher or lower than average results in accordance with the test subject's decision is rare and variable, and is affected by the subject's general mood. When the subject is in a depressed mood and his level of concentration is low, he achieves results that are not statistically significant.

3. Some of the subjects with high telepathic ability were able to define the level of accuracy of their guesses prior to beginning the test, and determine whether they would achieve a significantly higher or lower than average result. When they were asked to concentrate and make a greater effort, and also when they were offered some kind of "incentive" (such as a sum of money), the results they achieved were higher than their personal average.

4. Mental factors such as stress, agitation, fatigue and depression significantly lowered the accuracy of the guesses of the people with unique abilities.

Other scientists reached Rhine's conclusion that the test results involve telepathic abilities, clairvoyance and predictive abilities. For this reason, the scientists attempted to isolate each of these properties and examine them separately. A transmitter and a receiver were set up to perform telepathic tests. The transmitter gazed at a picture, while the receiver tried to pick up what the transmitter was seeing. In clairvoyance tests, the subject had to gaze at the face-down cards when no one in the room, including the examiner, knew what was on the right side of the card. In prediction tests, the subject had to guess which sign would soon appear on the screen – just like Shackleton, who was able to guess which card would follow the one the examiner had revealed.

Psychokinesis

Psychokinesis is the ability to move objects or influence them or people with the power of thought. While various studies on telepathy and other extrasensory phenomena were conducted over the years and evoked a great deal of interest, the phenomena of telekinesis or psychokinesis were not formally investigated until the appearance of Uri Geller. In his performances, Geller turned these phenomena into phenomena whose existence could no longer be ignored. However, before we tell a few things about Uri Geller's astonishing feats, we will briefly survey the beginnings of the study of these phenomena in the Western world.

As early as 1853, the famous physician and chemist, Michael Farraday, investigated various psychokinetic phenomena. He reached his study topic indirectly. At that time, mediums were extremely fashionable, and the field of channeling with entities from the "other" world was expanding rapidly. Many mediums claimed that the spirits with whom they channeled caused various objects in the room to move – tables rising, objects floating, and so on. These claims made Michael Farraday wonder about the authenticity of the phenomena, and he began to study several mediums. Some of them turned out to be phonies who used diverse tricks in order to lift objects and create background noises that sounded like drumming or the rustle of spirits. However, Farraday discovered that some of the mediums actually did cause objects to move without any phony techniques. While Farraday could not determine unequivocally if it was spirits that moved the objects or the psychokinetic ability of the medium to move them with the power of thought, he was impressed by the fact that objects could in fact be moved by the power of thought, human or non-human. Michael Farraday was one of the first researchers to engage in the formal study of the phenomenon of psychokinesis.

After him, scientific interest in the phenomenon increased, even though it was still quite limited, since most broad-minded researchers who were interested in extra-sensory phenomena focused mainly on the study of tele-pathic phenomena. When scientific interest in psycho-kinesis began, the investigating scientists tried to devise various tests that would enable them to examine the existence of the phenomenon in as controlled a way as possible. Ingo Swann, one of the most famous subjects, impressed scientists with his ability to affect the temperature of water in a container.

He did this in a series of tests in which water was poured into two completely identical containers. A thermometer that was inserted into the water determined that the temperature of the water in both containers was absolutely identical. Swann concentrated, and ten minutes later, the water in one of the containers was ten degrees hotter than the water in the other container! In contrast to other subjects or actions of various mediums, Swann was able to repeat these amazing results in every one of the many tests he was asked to perform in the presence of a battery of various scientists and spectators. Swann reached the same astonishing result over and over again with the greatest of ease.

Another person who became famous for her unique abilities was Anna Rasmussen. In the tests she underwent, she had to influence the order of the illumination of light bulbs that were connected to a power source that conveyed an electrical current to the light bulbs in a completely random manner. The results were astounding. It transpired that Anna could influence the order in which the light bulbs lit up, sometimes to the point of 100% success.

The study of psychokinesis commenced officially with the work of the famous researcher, Prof. Joseph Rhine. In the 1930s, Rhine tried to examine scientifically the effect of thought on objects. Concurrently with his in-depth research of this topic, he was fortunate to receive unexpected help and acquire a fascinating research subject. Tom Beades, a young man and a gambler, approached him with the intention of demonstrating his telekinetic abilities – the way he influenced the die and directed it to show the number he wanted!

The best-known story about Tom Beades took place in the casino of a Las Vegas hotel. The place was crowded with excited, adrenaline-filled people gambling at the one-armed bandits and the gaming tables.

That day, young Tom Beades lost everything he owned – all the money he had saved up went down the drain. The lust for gambling had been too powerful and uncontrolled, and Tom had not managed to stop in time. Now he was penniless. Desperate, depressed, anguished and stunned, he walked to the bathroom, oblivious of the people around him. While he was washing his face, which was shining with the cold sweat of the anxiety that had gripped him when he had failed so dismally, he glimpsed a five-dollar chip lying under the sink. He picked it up. The chip was worth so little – what could he do with it? But in Tom's penniless situation, he saw the chip as a sign – a sign from heaven. He clutched it tightly in his fist, and strode with determination to the gaming tables. He stopped at one of the tables and waited impatiently for a place to come free so that he could place the bet. When a place came free, Tom placed the chip on number seven. The dice-thrower began to shake the dice in a special cup. Tom muttered to himself, "Seven. It must be seven now." The dice-thrower threw the dice onto the table, and the numbers three and four appeared in front of Tom's eyes. He swept up the chips he had won, and quickly placed them on another number. Once more, his lips moved in a kind of silent prayer, and his eyes stared at the dice, as if he were hypnotizing them. Again, the number he had gambled on came up. He continued gambling until his pocket contained a sum of money that not only covered all his losses, and but gave him huge profits as well. Astonished and admiring people watched him as he finally left the table, the expression on his face indifferent and not betraying what was going on in his heart. Two girls tried to attract his attention, clutching at his arms so that he would invite them to have a "good time," but Tom ignored them and slipped away quickly. He hurried over to a bank to deposit his winnings. Withdrawn and serious, he walked to his room in the modest hotel where he was staying. He extracted a pair of dice from among his belongings. Concentrating and silent, he began to roll them on the floor, staring at the numbers that came up.

Two weeks later, he arrived at Prof. Rhine's office at

Duke University. Prof. Rhine, who was conducting many studies on telepathy at the time, was prepared to listen to the surprising words of the 30-year-old man who had come into his office. The quiet words uttered by the man were to have a tremendous effect on the development of the study of telekinesis. "I'm a gambler," said Tom Beades, "and I can influence the dice with the power of thought. The number I choose is the number that comes up when the die is cast."

From that day on, for ten fascinating years, Prof. Rhine investigated the astounding phenomenon that Tom Beades had presented to him. In his lengthy research, the professor studied the ability of certain people to convert thought energy into kinetic energy – the energy of movement – thereby influencing moving objects, such as dice, as they pleased.

Prof. Rhine performed many experiments with dice because they were very convenient for the aim of the research. When two dice are thrown, the resulting totals range between 2 and 12. There are 36 possible combinations. Prof. Rhine divided up the chances as follows: There are 15 possibilities of getting a total of 8 or more, 15 possibilities of getting a total of 6 or less, and 6 possibilities of getting a 7. After eliminating the parameter of the person's influence on the dice by using a special machine to cast the dice, it is possible to work out the proportion, in a large number of throws, between the results of 8 and above, 6 and below, and 7.

During the research, when a person throws the dice a certain number of times, and there is an upward or downward deviation from the above-mentioned proportion after checking the machine-cast dice, this means that somehow a certain influence was exerted on the dice, thereby changing the proportion between the various groups of results. How does this deviation occur? Is it possible that with the power of thought, or with strong will power, the person can influence the results of a throw of the dice? This was the question that bewitched and bothered Prof. Rhine, and he was determined to find an answer.

For ten years, with the help of students and his research team, Prof. Rhine performed numerous dice-throwing experiments. These studies showed that certain people, consistently and non-coincidentally, could direct the dice to show results of above or below 7 when throwing two dice. This ability disrupted the existing proportionality between the number of the various groups of results attained from machine-cast dice.

However, despite this impressive finding, Prof. Rhine still feared the objections of his scientific colleagues as well as the reaction of the public to his research. He felt that the results of his studies had to be even clearer and more unequivocal in order for them to be received with understanding rather than with an endless stream of rejection and opposition. He continued devising new tests for throwing the dice in order to investigate the influence of the subject's power of thought or will power on the results of the throw of the dice.

Another unique study was conducted by means of a unique machine, which cast the dice onto a board that was divided in two by a line along its length. The subject's aim was to try to influence the dice to roll further away from one side of the line than from the other. "Rationally" speaking, there is no any reason for the dice to roll further on one side of the divided board. There should not be any clear and non-random difference in the distances. But, surprisingly, it turned out that certain people, using their power of thought or will power, could get the dice to roll further on one of the sections of the board. The number of cases in which this unique phenomenon occurred and the consistency with which certain people could repeat the "trick" over and over again, removed any suspicion of coincidence.

During the course of his research, Prof. Rhine discovered that there were additional parameters that influenced the results of the experiments and their success. These parameters were dependent on the human factor – the urge that motivated the person to succeed in the test and the level of his personal interest, such as a tempting sum of money that he was offered if he succeeded in obtaining the desired result. This parameter turned out to be extremely important, since many of the people who were able to "control" the movement of the dice were far more successful when they had a clear personal motive to do so.

After ten years of experiments, discoveries and insights in the field of psychokinesis, Prof. Rhine decided to publish the results of his research and its procedure. Since they were in-depth and firmly based, they were received with great faith and with ever-increasing interest both by his scientific colleagues and the general public.

However, the person who brought the wonderful field of psychokinesis "out of the closet" was the renowned Uri Geller. Studies that appear in scientific journals or even in popular magazines exert a certain effect on the reader and arouse his interest. But when a person has the opportunity to see the results of psychokinesis with his own eyes, via his TV set, or even more than that – to feel the influence of the power of thought on objects in his home – the effect is far greater.

Even before his big public appearance on British television in 1973, Uri Geller was known for his telekinetic abilities. However, his appearance on the British TV program was stunning. During a live broadcast, Uri Geller bent forks and succeeded in reviving watches that had stopped working. Among other impressive feats that demonstrated his amazing telekinetic abilities, he stopped Big Ben, disrupted the computer system of a large German publishing network, and influenced objects in the homes of TV viewers – objects moved and floated, "dead" watches suddenly started working, and cutlery became bent and crooked. Uri Geller did all this in front of the TV cameras and in the presence of other people.

A close friend of mine told me about a personal experience that occurred at the end of the 1960s in Israel. Several curious friends suggested that she go with them to a performance by Uri Geller in Tel Aviv. She was not particularly impressed with Uri Geller and thought that he was a phony. She felt that the whole idea of telekinesis was a particularly successful magician's trick, a kind of illusion that had no bearing on reality. She was sure that Uri Geller "pulled strings" offstage, planted certain people in the audience, and used watches and forks that he had prepared beforehand, somehow making them easy to bend so that his "tricks" would succeed on stage. Despite the contempt she felt for "the Uri Geller phenomenon," she was quite happy to have a night out with her friends. While she was in the auditorium, she watched the performance with great skepticism, but she had to admit to herself that it was enjoyable and quite fascinating. Having said that, she could not keep her suspicions to herself, and every now and then insisted on bothering her friends with her ideas about how the guy she considered a charlatan succeeded in pulling the wool over the eyes of the audience. When Uri Geller requested a female volunteer who was wearing a ring that did not mean much to her come up onto the stage, her friends pushed her, pointed at her, and created a slight commotion, until she was forced to go up. Geller looked at the rings on her fingers and asked her if she was prepared to "sacrifice" one of them. He promised her that afterwards she would receive a sum of money equal to the value of the ring so that she could purchase a new one. Curious, the girl pointed at the gold ring she had bought recently. It was not an expensive or special ring, and she agreed to "risk" it. Deep inside, she thought that now the cat was out of the bag. She didn't believe that anything would happen to her ring. Geller asked her to take off the ring, hold it in her hand, and make a fist. She held the ring in her closed fist. Geller concentrated and made a few movements over her closed fist. She felt heat and a strange sensation in her hand. When he instructed her to open her hand, the ring was broken in two equal pieces. She knew very well that there was no way that she had broken her gold ring with the strength of her fist.

The amazing findings in the field of psychokinesis were not limited to psychology or entertainment only. As in the far-off days of Atlantis, when people had access to extrasensory knowledge and insights as well as a more developed ability to use those powers, there were people who searched for ways to exploit these findings for their personal benefit, even if this was generally considered manipulative and immoral.

In the USSR, researchers of psychokinesis took another step forward (and, we might add, from the point of view of mankind, a step backward...). Through simple logic, they reached the conclusion that if a person has the ability to influence objects with the power of thought, he can also influence various weapons – not to mention other people – with the power of thought. But before we become acquainted with the Soviet attempts to use the power of thought for bellicose and manipulative purposes, it is interesting to examine the experiment of the Czech researcher, Robert Pavelita, to use the thought inspiration ability on inanimate objects.

The fact that human beings can cause deviations in the results of die throws, turn on particular light bulbs in a device with a random electrical current, or bend teaspoons, inspired various theories among scientists. One of the theories stated that certain people can convert low-tension physical energy in their brains into high- tension psychic energy, and vice versa. Robert Pavelita began to work on the practical side of these theories. He built several small appliances that he called "psychotronic generators." The objective of these appliances was to store human mental energy and to release it for particular purposes. Actually, what Pavelita did was to charge various inanimate objects – paper, wood, wool, and so on – with energy that could serve a variety of purposes: curing and healing on the one hand and exterminating pests on the other!

Pest extermination was one of the topics on which Pavelita concentrated in his research. He focused on this topic because it had extensive applied and commercial potential, so that even if the scientific community rejected the results of his research, it could bear fruit commercially.

In the 1970s, the experimental tests in the field of pest extermination commenced, with the help of the psychotronic generators. It turned out that these generators really could exterminate pests in the fields! However, the side effects that accompanied the success of the experiments eliminated any possibility of marketing the generators for pest extermination.

It transpired that in addition to exterminating pests, the generators caused more serious phenomena among human beings – anxiety attacks, heart attacks, thought neutralization, strange and disturbing sensations, and more. Having said that, the Czech researchers attained considerable success in other fields with the activation of the generators, in which the results were not so dangerous as they had been with pest extermination. They managed to move various objects by means of the psychotronic generators, to move the hands of clocks, and so on.

The American government, well aware both of the similar experiments performed by the Soviets and the danger inherent in these abilities (for instance, the potential of the generators to activate warheads or explosives from a distance), wasted no time in becoming actively involved in these studies. With surprising frankness, one of the members of the American Atomic Energy Commission admitted that the US was deeply interested in topics such as securing nuclear weapons by extrasensory means and activating and deactivating missiles by means of telekinesis. Several years after the Czech group commenced its experiments in charging objects and telekinesis, American researchers sponsored by the government joined in.

A more beneficial and straightforward experiment in

charging objects is being conducted nowadays by the parapsychologist, David Ashdown, and a small group of researchers in the field of physics. Following many years of research, this group succeeded in creating a unique method of charging various objects with energy for purposes of curing and healing. Prominent among the unique energetically-charged objects invented by the group are the prints called "vibrations." The vibrations are sheets of paper on which computer-processed printing appears. The energy-charged vibrations create opening, healing, soothing, or stimulating sensations.

Moreover, every unique vibration has a particular range of shapes and colors, which have a mental and energetic effect on the person who looks at them and touches them. The success of the energy-charged vibrations has not yet been subjected to testing by a battery of scientists and researchers, but the recording of the results of the effect of the vibrations on a broad range of people indicates considerable success.

Dreams

In a state of full consciousness, there are many emotional and rational barriers, most of which are unconscious, that block the reception of telepathic emissions or the recognition of extrasensory phenomena that may occur in everyday life. The inner "chatting" processes that accompany many people are generally normal processes. They include a "replay" of conversations, events, and situations that we experience, have experienced, or want to experience, "staged" conversations between the person and people who play a part in his life (sometimes, even in the street, we can see people holding conversations of this kind with themselves; their lips sometimes move slightly and their body language hints that they are involved in some kind of "conversation" with themselves), imaginings, daydreams, plans, and sometimes just everyday stress that is linked to routine chores. These processes are completely natural and familiar to most people. However, in a person who is not especially attuned to and aware of subconscious and extrasensory processes, they are liable to block the reception of extrasensory messages or prevent him from understanding the messages concealed behind seemingly ordinary everyday phenomena. In the chapter on telepathy, we mentioned the fact that all of humankind is connected in a broad telepathic net that seemingly enables us (if we know how to use this "net") to pick up many messages, especially from people who are close to us, but also from people to whom we are connected and linked in a stronger way. However, because of the emotional and rational occupations during the day, many of these messages evade our consciousness. This is not the case when we sleep.

Because of the unique state of awareness that occurs when we dream, the dream constitutes a broad cushion for picking up various cosmic messages. These may be telepathic messages that reach us in various guises, in a certain translation, or even directly, prophetic dreams, symbolic dreams, and even dreams whose objective is to process and review various impressions that emerge from our subconscious. They may be impressions that were absorbed during the day, or even in past years, and are "published" when the state of consciousness enables them to manifest themselves.

Since the dream state is a different state of consciousness, in which imagination and reality, past, present and future as well as various images and situations are all mixed up without the limitations of the recognized laws of reality, dreams have always evoked a great deal of interest – both in ancient times and cultures and in the modern era. Because of the mysterious covering that accompanies many dreams, various mystical contexts, superstitions, and even prophetic contexts have been attributed to dreams. In contrast, the many processes of rationalization that appeared in the 18th, 19th and 20th centuries contributed to the creation of psychological theories that attempted to explain the nature and meaning of dreams.

Attempts to understand the dream states were already made in ancient times. Especially famous is the story of one of the wise men of the Mishnah who got into a conversation about dreams with a Greek general who was in the Land of

Israel at the time. Speaking from a profound psychological understanding, the wise man told the general that he would dream of being assassinated that night. He elaborated on the details of the dream that the general would allegedly dream. The next day, the general, upset and scared, admitted that his dream had been exactly as the rabbi said it would be. He was very surprised and assumed that the wise man could "see the future" and knew what he would dream. However, this was not the case. As the wise man explained to him afterwards, the act of "brainwashing," the persuasion and the suggestion, the manner of describing the dream to the general – all these things caused the dream to actually occur. In fact, many dreams are "vain speech" – that is, dreams that involve motives from everyday life that bother us when we are awake, bring to the conscious level conflicts and anxieties, hopes and sometimes even things that were read in newspapers or viewed on TV. At night, these things are released from the subconscious, sometimes as a way of relieving the tension that is created by unconscious conflicts or anxieties. Although these dreams are not essentially prophetic or telepathic, they are very important, since they can teach us a great deal about ourselves.

Some dreams occur in order to make us aware of various things – such as fears or hidden passions that are bothering us – which we do not allow to rise to the conscious level. When such a repressing mechanism is activated in daily life, a symbolic dream may occur, which describes the repressed feeling. The most widespread of this type of dream is the falling dream, the drowning dream, the fleeing dream, and so on, whose purpose is to describe a feeling to which the person does not related sufficiently in everyday life, but certainly bothers him unconsciously. Symbolic dreams are also very important, and the ability to remember them and process them consciously can contribute greatly to knowing oneself and developing one's personality.

Thus, when we deal with dreams in this book, we will relate to them on two planes – the symbolic dream, or the bridging dream (a dream that bridges between the repressing conscious and the subconscious, in which the repressed situation is alive and active), and the telepathic and prophetic dream.

Understanding symbolic dreams and bridging dreams is very important in the practical training of extrasensory ability. The ability to be aware of what is going on around us but does not reach us via the "conventional" senses (the senses of sight, hearing, and so on) is greatly dependent on our ability to introspect and be aware of what is happening inside us. The greater the amount of repressed inner content, and the more blocked the bridge between the conscious and the subconscious, the smaller the chance of developing extrasensory abilities or extrasensory perception (except for people with an "innate" ability, or an ability that is sparked suddenly following an extremely significant event). For this reason, it is very important to remember and understand dreams. Later on, we will present several methods for remembering dreams and for gaining insights concerning dreams whose meaning is not clear. Other very powerful tools for understanding and remembering dreams (in addition to self-awareness and intuition, of course) are the various crystals, because they are very effective and easy to use, and do not require extensive study, exhausting practice or exceptional talents.

As opposed to symbolic and bridging dreams, there are

telepathic and prophetic dreams. Prophetic dreams are familiar to us from many stories and legends. The Bible is full of such dreams – Joseph's dreams, Pharaoh's dreams, Jacob's dream, and so on. The prophetic dream is a tool for receiving a cosmic message, and it served many prophets, visionaries, clairvoyants, as well as artists and scientists. Prophetic dreams dreamed by creators and researchers are known to be closely linked to the person's research topic or occupation. Since every person has a vocation in this world, people who have found their vocation or who delve deeply into a certain topic may receive many clues and insights regarding their field of occupation via dreams. Many people who are involved in religion, the humanities and the sciences used this kind of channeling dream and prophetic dream for their work. Although some of them were very rational people and some of them lived in eras when no importance was attributed to dreaming in its mystical sense, they knew how to use dreams for their own benefit. Sometimes, from a deep insight that the unique abilities they possessed in this world came from something "greater" than could be perceived and absorbed by the senses, these people knew, consciously or unconsciously, how to "order" dreams that would provide them with information or inspiration concerning the issues in which they were engaged. One of the most famous of these "dreamers" was Rabbi Jacob of Marvish, a Kabbalist and one of the greatest 12th-century French Hasids, who wrote a whole book about Halachic questions and responses based on information that came to him while he was dreaming! The field of the Halacha, which he dealt with, was widely considered to be a logical and rational field, in which one thing had to be deduced from another by means of logical reasoning and intellectual analysis. Having said that, however, the book he wrote, like his responses that became renowned among the Halachic sages, was accepted unequivocally. Rabbi Jacob of Marvish was in the habit of asking Halachic questions that had been addressed to him during prayer, while linking up to holy names and the names of angels, and he would receive the answers at night in his dreams!

Friedrich Kekule, a well-known German chemist who discovered the molecular structure of benzene, grappled with the problem for a long time without reaching the desired results. He received the answer to the question that had been irking him for days and nights via a dream while he was sleeping. He saw a snake biting its own tail. This vision joined up with all the information he had already discovered, thereby enabling him to discover the molecular structure he had been struggling to find for so long. Albert Einstein, too, admitted that some of the equations he solved had been revealed to him in dreams.

Prophetic dreams can occur during situations of distress or when disasters are about to befall the person himself or the people close to him. The sinking of the *Titanic*, for instance, sparked prophetic dreams in many relatives of people who perished in the disaster. Many of them related that they had received clues or visions in dreams prior to the sinking.

A fascinating story involving this kind of dream occurred in October 1965, in the Welsh village of Aberfen. A sudden collapse of a slag dump buried 128 children and teachers in the village school. A week before the event, a woman from Sidcup in Kent dreamed about the disaster. Another woman, from Aylesbury in Buckinghamshire, dreamed about the disaster two days before it occurred, and a day before the actual event, one of the children at the school told her mother that she had dreamed she was going to school, but instead of seeing the school building, all she saw was black stuff covering the entire school area.

History is full of reliable testimonies of seeing the future through dreams. The interesting thing is that in most cases, although the dream attempted to announce something and get the relevant parties to talk about their predictive dream – even when the dreamer dreamed about something that was liable to happen to himself – in some strange way, the disaster was not averted.

World War I began with the unexpected assassination of the Archduke Franz Ferdinand of the Austro-Hungarian Empire. In this case, the information reached a man who himself was of high standing – Bishop Joseph Lanay. In his dream, Lanay saw the archduke riding on his horse along a Sarajevo street, when he was suddenly slain by a bullet from a pistol. Taking no chances, Lanay hurried to send a telegram to the Archduke – but the latter was assassinated before the telegram reached its destination!

The American president, Abraham Lincoln, was assassinated by actor John Wilkes Booth while watching a play. A few days prior to the assassination, the president had a particularly disturbing dream. In his dream, he saw himself walking through the White House. When he reached the East Wing, his eyes espied a corpse lying on the funerary platform. In his dream, Lincoln asked the guards who the dead man was. They answered, "It's the president; he was murdered by an assassin." This dream did not prevent the actual event, either.

Telepathic dreams

Telepathic dreams are another kind of extrasensory phenomenon that occurs in dreams. In various cultures, there is a belief that dreams originate in a "whisper" of the spirit of a dead person who is related or linked to the dreamer, or in a tie that is created between the dreamer and a certain figure that communicates with him, and transmits its messages to him via the dream.

Sometimes, telepathic dreams are dreamed simultaneously by two closely linked people.

There are many stories about telepathic dreams in which a person dreams about something that happens to someone close to him who is far away from him physically. Sometimes, the dream occurs at the same time as the event that concerns the person he dreamed about. Such dreams are not rare, and may occur in people whose ability to link up to their surroundings, that is, their ability for spiritual openness and reception, is especially high, consciously or unconsciously.

Modern studies have attempted to examine whether it is really possible to convey telepathic messages to the dreamer while he is asleep. One of the most common ways for conducting these studies was to transmit telepathic messages to the sleeper while he was asleep. Generally speaking, the transmitter received a picture and began to concentrate on it, while the receiver was sleeping and linked up to electrodes that measured his brainwaves. The researchers waited until the measurement of the brainwaves and of the rapid eye movements signaled that the sleeping receiver was dreaming, and woke him up immediately after the dream. Frequently, the dreamer was able to describe the picture that the transmitter concentrated on as a part of his dream, as a picture, or as a detail that got mixed up in his dream. Several scientists claimed that this experiment was not reliable, and there was a chance that the dreamer could guess what the transmitter had transmitted to him. In order to make the experiment more reliable, the researchers used five Zener cards or five animal cards that are used in telepathic experiments.

By using these cards, the chance of a random guess was one out of five, that is, a 20% chance of a correct guess. In experiments performed in France, the level of guessing the cards reached 55%, far beyond any possibility of a random guess. Later on, we will describe an easy method for conducting these experiments at home, with a partner.

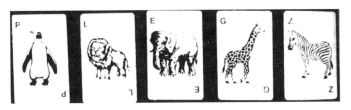

Animal cards used in telepathic experiments.

However, beyond the scientific experiments for telepathic revelation while dreaming, the stories about unique telepathic messages received by sleeping people from relatives are especially fascinating. Like prophetic dreams, many of these telepathic messages occurred when a person close to the dreamer was in some kind of danger.

Another amazing story linked to the sinking of the *Titanic* tells of the brother of one of the ship's sailors. The brother woke up in the middle of the night, sweating and shaken, having seen his brother drowning in the ocean. The brother, who was on the deck of the *Titanic*, was fighting the waves exactly at the time when his brother saw him drowning in his dream!

Telepathic occurrences between siblings in dreams are not rare. The blood ties and the link between the souls that causes two people to be born as siblings in this incarnation are so powerful that the distress of one of the siblings can appear in the dreams of the other siblings.

The author, Mark Twain, told of a shocking nightmare he had had. In his dream, he saw a large hall containing a metal coffin that was lying on two chairs. When he approached and peeped inside the coffin, he saw the body of his brother. On his dead brother's chest was a bunch of white flowers, among which there was a single red flower.

At the time, Mark Twain's brother was serving on the ship, the *Pennsylvania*.

Mark Twain was aware of the power of dreams. Various parts of his books, as well as his ideas for writing, occurred more than once in his dreams. He had a hard time forgetting the dream the next day, and his heart presaged bad news. And so it was. That same day, he was informed that an explosion on the deck of the *Pennsylvania* caused the death of 150 crewmen – among them his brother.

In pain and sorrow, Mark Twain noticed, on the day of the funeral, how similar the image of the coffin in his dream was to the real coffin in which his brother was lying. Everything was so similar – only the bunch of flowers he had seen in his dream was missing. Suddenly, a woman entered the funeral parlor, holding a bunch of white flowers, with a single red flower in the middle!

Telepathy

The famous Prof. Rhine, who conducted extensive research on extrasensory phenomena, told a story that he had heard from one of his professors when he himself was a young student. The professor related an event that had occurred during his childhood. One night, the professor's family woke up in a fright to the sound of loud banging on the door. One of their neighbors, panicked and terrified, burst in and begged them to lend her their carriage. They tried to calm the frightened woman down – she looked as if she had just woken up. Her hair was wild, and her eyes were full of fear. But she would not calm down, and demanded that they make their carriage available to her, since she had just awoken from a terrible dream. She saw her brother, on another farm, committing suicide in the barn. Immediately, they prepared the carriage for her, and she set out for her brother's farm. When she returned, broken and grieving, she told them that when she went into the barn, she found her brother lying dead in a pool of his own blood after shooting himself.

As we have said, dreams are an extremely important tool for developing awareness and extrasensory perception. Since some of them are messages from other dimensions, even when they occur as a result of things that happen in the subconscious world, they develop our ability to listen to messages from dimensions other than the physical-concrete dimension in which we live. The first step toward developing the ability to dream and the ability to receive messages in dreams is, of course, the ability to remember dreams.

Psychometry

Psychometry is the ability to sense the vibrations that emanate from a particular object, thereby channeling or sensing the owner of the object. People with psychometric powers can grasp an object that belongs to a missing person, for instance, and, upon entering a meditative state or a trance, can see the things that befell the owner of the object by means of clairvoyance that is frequently combined with a supernatural sensory ability and intuitive knowledge. Many police forces throughout the world make use of people with these powers in order to locate missing persons, to reconstruct murders, or to obtain impressions and information about criminals who left some kind of personal object behind at the scene of the crime. This is one of the extrasensory abilities that is most widely used professionally, and generally speaking, the person with psychometric powers is consulted after all the other directions of investigation have reached a dead end. Although there are not many unequivocal scientific findings regarding psychometry because the topic has not yet been studied extensively, police detectives and investigators, as well as private individuals who face mysteries that cannot be solved in a conventional manner, do not hesitate to turn to these people.

Arthur Young, the inventor of the helicopter rotor, tried to figure out what had caused the helicopter accident in which the pilot and copilot had been killed. Suffering severe guilt feelings, he searched in vain for the technical flaw that had caused the accident. Despite his prodigious technical knowledge, he did not find an answer. Finally, he brought a fragment of the helicopter's propeller to the famous medium, Eileen Grant. Grant held the fragment in her hands, and, using her psychometric abilities, tried to see what had occurred during the accident. She said that the accident had not been caused by a technical flaw, but rather by the pilot himself, who had been on the verge of a nervous breakdown at the time. She explained that the pilot had just decided to make a drastic change in his lifestyle – he was planning to enter a monastery. Young did not feel that he had the emotional strength to interrogate and question the grieving family of the deceased, and although the medium's words eased his conscience somewhat and provided him with a measure of relief, he could not be completely sure of their veracity. A year after that meeting, he met the director of the agency that had hired the pilot. During the meeting, the director told him in a low voice, as if he were revealing a deep secret, that the pilot had indeed been on the verge of a nervous breakdown and was considering entering a monastery.

The use of supernatural abilities for "detective work" is one of the most widespread ways of using these abilities. Gerard Kreust, the famous Dutch medium, became widely renowned as a result of cooperating with the police in numerous cases of locating missing and kidnapped persons.

"The case of Liliane"

The following case was examined and endorsed by the French Metaphysical Institute, which is considered to be the highest authority on matters of the supernatural.

Liliane disappeared from her home in the suburbs of Paris without any prior notice or indication of her whereabouts. In the hopes of finding their daughter, her parents asked the medium, Raymond Riant, to meet with them. He agreed to help them, and they brought him a picture of Liliane and a dress that belonged to her in order to help him make contact with her.

During the first sitting, Riant saw Liliane safe and sound traveling in a train with a friend somewhere in northern France.

During the second sitting, Riant described what he saw: "Liliane is sitting on a bench in an old building that looks like a police building in Paris. A blonde girl is sitting next to her. Liliane is spending the night in what looks like a detention cell. I don't see her friend with her."

During the third sitting, Riant said: "The girls are hitching a ride. They are in a region of hills and valleys that looks a bit like Normandy. The girls want to get into a small motorboat. Liliane is wearing a black polo-neck sweater. The location I received by using a pendulum is the Helder district in Holland."

A few days later, Raymond Riant described Liliane's return to Paris, and followed her movements right up to the point when she returned to her parents' home.

After her parents told her what they had gone through during her absence, Liliane told them what had happened to her, and her father completed her sentences with the details he knew.

Liliane had run away from home in the direction of Paris with her friend Claudine. After wandering around for some time, she was arrested for attempting to steal jewelry. They had indeed hitchhiked to Amsterdam. That same day, they got into a small motorboat in order to get to north Amsterdam, to the Helder district. She was in fact wearing a polo-neck sweater that day, but it was beige, not black.

Liliane was astounded at the way her father described the events she had gone through, and although she tried to conceal her arrest, he told her confidently how she had spent the night in a detention cell, and demanded to know why. She was sure that her parents had hired detectives to follow her.

This case, which was investigated and documented, shows the amazing level of accuracy that a skilled and talented medium can reach. Riant could describe Liliane's activities, the places in which she was, and even whom she was with.

"The Drummond case"

This case was presented in a book and its authenticity was confirmed by police investigators who participated in the investigation.

Mr. Drummond, a man who had passed middle age, went camping with his wife. He decided to take a short stroll, a brief hike after which he would return to their little camp. He was supposed to return within a half-hour to an hour, but he was absent for much longer. After a day of waiting, his anxious and worried wife turned to the local sheriff and asked him to help her locate her husband. The search began, and when there was no sign of Mr. Drummond, many people volunteered to join in. After two weeks of searching and over 300 people participating in the extensive search, there was still no sign of Mr. Drummond. Six months after the incident, when the police had already given up hope of finding him, Mrs. Drummond contacted Kathleen Rea, a medium who had become renowned for helping the police solve numerous cases. Kathleen Rea recorded a 40-minute cassette in which she described her feelings regarding Mr. Drummond's disappearance. She said that Mr. Drummond had completely lost his sense of direction, and had begun to walk in an easterly direction. She described a dirt road that went by a hut in the middle of a grove of trees. She went on to say that as soon as he had taken this road, he had had a heart attack, and had collapsed behind some large thorn-bushes in the grove. She claimed that his body was still there, and, surprisingly, was still completely intact. Mrs. Drummond brought the tape to the sheriff, who decided to try to find the place with the help of his deputy before organizing another search party. Kathleen Rea's descriptions were so accurate that the authorities located the avenue of trees next to the hut easily; behind a clump of tangled thorn-bushes lay Mr. Drummond's body. After that, the deputy sheriff declared that Kathleen Rea's descriptions on the 40-minute tape were almost completely accurate.

Astral travel

Try to remember whether this experience is familiar to you. You come home after an exhausting day's work, spend a few hours in front of the TV, and feel drowsiness enveloping you. You turn off the TV, shuffle tiredly toward the bedroom, and expect to fall asleep in a few minutes. However, suddenly and mysteriously, you find your body paralyzed. Noises echo in your ears, flashes of bright light pass through your closed eyes. And then you feel as if you are beginning to float. A moment later, you open your eyes, and find yourself floating above your body. You are really floating in the air – and you can look down at your body and gaze at it, and you can look at everything in your room and see what is happening there. You do not feel judgmental or worried – it seems as if your brain has been completely liberated from the limits of the body and the subjective mind, and you feel a sense of expanded awareness, and a kind of feeling of freedom and lightness. And as you begin to understand and wonder about the nature of the situation you find yourself in, you experience a blackout of a fraction of a second, and then you "wake up," and find yourself inside your body, lying in your bed.

If this experience sounds familiar to you, you have experienced astral travel. This experience is not so rare, and many people have it, even if they do not know that it should be defined as an "out-of-body experience."

In astral travel, the astral body leaves the physical body. The astral body is one of the seven energetic bodies that exist around the physical body.

Certain people can go off on astral travels naturally. Others are afraid of leaving the physical body and fight against it, so they do not succeeded in going on astral travel.

In astral travel, we remain linked to our body and to this dimension by means of a silver cord (like the umbilical cord) that joins the astral body to the physical body, but we cannot always see it. During the course of astral travel, the person may reach different places, different dimensions of awareness. He may visit some place in the present – and be there while things occur (mainly places where there are people who are dear to him or places where he has a special interest in the events that are occurring there), or some place in the past or the future, which exists in other dimensions. Many people describe seeing temples or unfamiliar holy places during their astral travel. Sometimes, when the astral travel commences, a white horse or a black panther appears, symbolizing the beginning of the journey.

Stories about various kinds of spiritual journeys that we are supposed to consider as astral travel can be found in many ancient writings. In most cases, the attitude toward these cases resembled the attitude toward folk legends. However, one of the cases that changed the somewhat derisive perception of astral travel was the publication of the experience of the British scientist, Oliver Fox.

One afternoon in 1913, in a quiet London suburb, Oliver Fox was dozing in his room. He had not yet sunk into his afternoon nap when he began to feel his spirit leaving his body and going through his bedroom without opening the door, going out and evaporating, weightless and transparent, through the heavy metal door at the entrance to his house.

Fox found himself in the street. He passed along the street where he lived, and was swept, or perhaps pulled, to a small and pleasant park that he had never visited. He saw several children playing in the park and some people having a picnic, but continued moving onward until he reached a quiet residential area. The front door of one of the houses was open. Fox went inside, wondering if anyone in the house would sense his presence. Since there was no one on the ground floor, he moved up the carpeted flight of stairs to the second floor of the house. There he entered a room that looked like a bedroom. A young, good-looking woman sat on a low chair opposite a dressing-table mirror, combing her hair. She did not seem to sense his presence. He advanced toward her and stood behind her. The image of the young woman appeared in the mirror, combing her long hair – but Fox's reflection did not appear in the mirror! At that moment, he realized that he could see but was unseen. He wondered: Can the woman discern my presence? She does not see me, but can she sense me? He placed his hand on the woman's bare shoulder and could feel the softness of her skin beneath his fingers. Suddenly a violent shock-wave passed through the woman's body and there was terror in her eyes. At that moment, Fox felt his body swept far away from the room, and he woke up lying in his bed.

As in the case of telepathy, the out-of-body experience attracted scientists and researchers to examine the topic in depth. In his book, *Leaving the Body*, Scott Rogo, from

Kennedy University in California, presents many studies dealing with the out-of-body experience. One of the first studies on this matter was conducted at the beginning of the 1950s by Dr. Hornell Hart, a sociologist from Duke University in North Carolina. Dr. Hart asked 155 students about the out-of-body experience, and discovered that 27% of them had had at least one out-of-body experience in their lives. During the 1960s, Celia Green conducted an identical study in England. She randomly chose 115 students from the University of Southampton. Nineteen percent of them admitted that they had had an out-of-body experience. When Green conducted a similar study with 380 students from Oxford University, 34% of the responders began to talk about their out-of-body experiences! Studies that have been performed in recent years provided similar findings. After many studies of this kind, performed either with university students or with different groups throughout the world, Scott Rogo makes the well-founded assumption that one out of every five people has had at least one out-of-body experience in his life. This is a relatively enormous number for an extrasensory experience, and it shows the out-of-body experience to be a fairly common experience. The experience can occur under various circumstances and in a broad range of situations.

In old occult writings, the experience was described as mystical and unique, and sometimes even as dangerous. In contrast, in studies that were conducted in recent years, it transpired that the experience is so widespread that it might be one of the qualities that exist in all human beings, and it is possible to learn or acquire the art of voluntarily activating the experience. In inquiries and debriefings that were conducted among people of different age-groups and personality structures, it was found that most of them described the experience as "pleasant and liberating," and many of them were prepared to undergo it again. Many people who had this experience in a natural way did not dabble in the occult or belong to any kind of New Age trend.

A researcher who investigated the matter in depth together with a relatively large group of well-known researchers from several universities in the United States, succeeded in finding several general characteristics of the out-of-body experience, based on the inquiries and debriefings of a large number of people who had undergone the experience. Seventy-nine percent of the responders who had had this experience had been in a calm emotional state and their bodies were relaxed when they had the experience spontaneously. The remaining 21% had a spontaneous experience while giving birth, as a result of the anesthetic, or as a result of fierce stabs of pain during an illness or a serious injury. Moreover, he found that people who practiced meditation displayed a great tendency to have spontaneous out-of-body experiences. The fact that 79% of the people who had had the experiences were not in any state of crisis, pain or distress may attest to the fact that the out-of-body experience is a normal human experience and not one that is caused by a severe crisis or a life-threatening situation, as was thought previously. Most of the responders said that they had heard a thundering in their ears, like waves of noise, before the beginning of the experience; they felt themselves "leaving their body" and saw their body remaining in the place it had been prior to the experience. Many passed through walls and ceilings during the extrasensory experience.

But the fact that astonished the researchers more than anything was the innocence of the responders regarding the experience. About one-third of the people who had experienced an out-of-body experience in no way expected such an experience, and many of them did not even know that such a thing existed. No less surprising is the fact that most of the people who underwent the experience enjoyed it! Eighty-five percent of the responders in a study that was performed in Kansas defined the experience as "pleasant," of them about half defined it as "extremely enjoyable." Likewise, it seems that the experience affected the world-view of many of the responders, as well as their views regarding life and death. About two-thirds of the responders said that the experience helped rid them of their fear of death and caused them to believe in life after death. Forty-three percent of the responders defined the experience as "the most awesome thing that has happened to me in my life." Most of them were keen to have more out-of-body experiences. Almost all the responders were certain that they had not been dreaming when they had undergone the experience.

The results of the Kansas study, which was performed by a group of psychiatrists, presented the three researchers with the following question: "Must the person who has the out-of-body experience possess special personality traits? Must he be 'different' in something than the rest of humanity?" Many researchers were interested in this question.

A questionnaire that was sent to the homes of the subjects who had undergone the experience helped the researchers answer the question. The researchers were looking for answers to questions such as: "Are people who undergo out-of-body experiences gifted with a more than normally active imagination?" "Are they more hysterical or neurotic than other people?" "Do they have a greater than normal ability to adapt?" After the questionnaires were handed in, it was simple to answer these questions. After checking the answers, the researchers reached the conclusion that people who had undergone out-of-body experiences were in no way different than people who had not!

These psychological findings are of great importance, since many psychiatrists tended to attribute the numerous stories of out-of-body experiences to various psychotic syndromes. After an in-depth study by the group of psychiatrists in Kansas and other researchers, it was concluded that the psychiatric syndromes to which various psychiatrists attempted to ascribe the experience were completely different, and the out-of-body experiences did not attest to any psychological or physical problem in the slightest.

Most astral travel experiences occur spontaneously, that is, sometimes even with people who are not at all aware of the possibility of leaving the body. In contrast, many experts claim that it is an ability that can be acquired, and there are even people who can go out on astral travel any time they so wish. The parapsychologist, Charles T., conducted one of his studies on the topic with a woman who could go out on astral travel "on demand." In the laboratory of T.'s parapsychology institute, the woman was hooked up to an ECG monitor in order to record her brain-waves, so that it would be possible to examine the states of brain-waves that enabled her to leave her body. After being hooked up to the machine, she was asked to perform a complicated exercise: if she actually could leave her body, as she claimed, she would have to identify the title of the book that was lying on a high shelf, near the ceiling. The woman succeeded in going out on astral travel by means of her will power, and identified the required title, even though her body did not move at all.

In the 1980s, I wanted to perform a similar experiment, without the use of an ECG monitor, on a person by the name of Robert Johnson, who claimed that he could go out on astral travel any time he wanted. I asked him to lie down on a mattress while I sat on a chair about 10 meters from him. When he had reclined and was beginning to prepare himself to relax his body, I wrote down five words in a notebook I was holding (in such a way that he could not see what I was writing) and I added three small drawings below them. I held the notebook in both hands, open, close to me. A few minutes after I finished writing and lifted up the notebook, I felt a strange sensation, a kind of discomfort behind my back. The person before me lay motionless and seemed to be asleep.

About 10 minutes later, Johnson sat up on the mattress. His eyes were turned toward me, but it looked as if he were staring at a picture in his memory. Within five seconds, he rapidly pronounced the five words. After a short pause, he described the three drawings and added that there was a spelling mistake in one of the words – I had written the letter E instead of the letter A. His accuracy was perfect.

One of the common reasons for the belief that astral travel occurs in states of distress or in situations in which the physical body cannot tolerate what is going on around it, stemmed from Ed Morrell's book, *The 25th Man*. As stated previously, in current studies, it has been found that only a relatively small percentage of out-of-body experiences originate from some kind of physical suffering or state of distress. Ed Morrell was an inmate of an Arizona prison about 60 years ago. During his four-year prison term, Morrell experienced extreme abuse at the hands of the wardens who conspired against him – physical violence and lengthy periods in cramped, dark solitary confinement. However, fortunately for Morrell, his soul found a way to get away from the physical tortures. Every time he spent a long time in solitary, Morrell would have an out-of-body experience, and his astral body would visit faraway and much more pleasant places. Morrell had good control of the direction and destinations of his visits during his out-of-body experiences. He could get to any place his soul desired and he met many people. After his release, he went to meet them and discovered that they really did exist in those places. Among other things, Morrell also met his future wife on his astral travels. In Morrell's case, when his terrible experiences in prison ended after he had been released and had begun to live a normal life, free of pain and pressure, his unique out-of-body experiences also ended.

In many cases of leaving the body, the person who is experiencing the astral travel relates to the astral body that leaves the physical body as a double. In such cases, the person himself is in a state of clear consciousness, which even enables him to channel with the "astral double" and receive messages and information from him. The famous French writer, Guy de Maupassant, related that occasionally, while he was writing one of his stories, his etheric double would "bother" him. This situation occurred relatively frequently with Maupassant, and he said that his double even dictated some of his most successful stories.

Certain stories about astral projections describe the presence of the etheric "double" in the company of friends and loved ones while the person himself was in another place. The Swedish playwright, Strindberg, deeply missed his family after he had moved to Paris following his divorce from his second wife. During those moments of profound yearning, his body floated to Sweden, where he lingered next to his mother-in-law, who was playing the piano, for a few minutes. Several days after the experience, Strindberg received a letter from his mother-in-law in which she wrote that she had seen his double that evening.

The English poet, Shelley, also experienced a projection of his astral body to a place where he longed to be. In an out-of-body journey, Shelley saw his etheric double in the company of Lord Byron and other friends while he himself was someplace else.

The American, Sylvan Muldoon, author of the book *Spotlight on the Astral Body* (published in 1921), described the following event in the journal, *The Occult Review* in 1931:

Mrs. B., an American, experienced astral journeys and could relate in detail what happened to her during these journeys. Most of the astral travel was involuntary, spontaneous, and generally occurred before dawn. Before actually leaving her body, Mrs. B. usually experienced a sensation of the physical dulling of the senses. The sensations that preceded the out-of-body experience included swift flashes of headache alternating with moments of a feeling of lightness. Her general feeling was that she had been caught in a powerful sweeping current. During the course of the out-of-body projection itself, Mrs. B. could not direct or navigate her astral body, but was conveyed involuntarily in a kind of sailing or floating manner. Uncharacteristically, her out-of-body experiences were accompanied by sensations of discomfort and pressure, distress, a feeling of suffocation, and sore throats. The unpleasant sensation would become stronger until it caused Mrs. B. to return to her body within a short time.

One of Mrs. B's journeys was unusual as compared to her other experiences. During the journey, she found herself in the parlor of a fancy house, luxurious and somewhat strange. From the living-room, her astral body floated up a staircase that was unique in its tremendous size, and from there, her astral body passed through an expansive hall into a room in which an elderly woman was lying. Mrs. B's astral body approached the old lady's bed with a kind of inexplicable hesitation – since she knew that during astral travel she was invisible. Suddenly, the old lady woke up, and it seemed that she could see Mrs. B! She looked into Mrs. B's face as if she was seeing a ghost. Mrs. B. describes her feeling at that moment: "I felt very embarrassed to be in that house, like a thief or a burglar, without an invitation. I moved backward with inexplicable fear, toward the winding spiral staircase, and instead of going down in a circular manner, I moved straight back. All at once, I felt myself falling down with a sharp sinking feeling in my stomach. Suddenly, a long whistle deafened me, and I found myself sitting in my bed, inside my physical body, breathless."

If it were possible to try to dismiss Mrs. B's experience as a dream or a fantasy, the events that occurred two years after this incident contradict that assumption. Mrs. B's cousin went to live in the town of Concord, about 60 kilometers from where Mrs. B. lived in New Hampshire. Her cousin had just purchased the house from the estate of an old lady whom Muldoon calls Mrs. M., who had died shortly before Mrs. B. went to visit her cousin. Mrs. B. had never seen her cousin's new house before. When she stood at the entrance to the house, a strange feeling came over her. A servant opened the door and led her to the parlor. The strange feeling became stronger in Mrs. B. and disturbed her. Her glance swept over the large space, which was somewhat familiar, and she had a powerful feeling that she had been there before. Only when her cousin came down the huge, winding staircase to greet her did Mrs. B. realize that this was the house she had visited during her astral journey. Afterwards, it transpired that the old lady who had seen Mrs. B. on her astral journey was none other than Mrs. M., whose house had been purchased by Mrs. B's cousin after her death.

The British researcher of extrasensory phenomena, Carrington, relates to Muldoon's stories with great faith and considers them to be a fascinating documentation that sheds light on the astonishing phenomenon. Muldoon, who, because of his many journeys and his documentation of them had been nicknamed "the astral traveler" in the United States, says that he could leave his physical body voluntarily and go out on journeys in his immediate surroundings and remain fully aware of what he was doing.

Muldoon's childhood had been spent in a house in which extrasensory phenomena were related to seriously. His mother was very interested in spiritualism, and when he was 12, she took him and his brother to a spiritualist camp in Iowa during the summer vacation. During their first night at the camp, Muldoon woke up with a feeling that he was somewhere else. He could not move his body, nor could he see or hear anything. It seemed as if his senses were not working. He only felt as if his body was floating, hovering up and down in the air rapidly, involuntarily, without his being able to control it. Suddenly he felt a blow on his head, and his body began to float in the air again, in zig-zag movements. While he was floating, his senses gradually began to function. The first sense to "return" to him was the sense of hearing, and after that his sense of sight also began to function once more. When he could see again, Muldoon identified his surroundings, and understood that he was floating near the ceiling of the house where he was staying the night with his mother and brother. He looked down and saw his physical body lying in the bed. He was anxious, because he was sure that he had died and that was why he could see his body below him, while he was ascending and floating near the ceiling. Instinctively, he hurried to wake his mother. He went to the second room and when he tried to open the door, it turned out that he was already on the other side! He had simply gone right through it. He went to his mother and touched her in order to rouse her, but she did not feel him at all. No one in the house sensed the frightened boy who was trying to wake them up with all his might. He felt that all his senses were functioning, except the sense of touch. He touched the sleeping people, tried to shake them – but they did not feel anything. The young Muldoon was shocked by the experience. He heard the wall clock chime twice – it was two o'clock in the morning. About 15 minutes after the chiming of the clock, Muldoon felt that he was being swept and drawn to his body in the bed, floating vertically in the air and rejoining his physical body. As he rejoined it, Muldoon woke up in his bed, covered in cold sweat and frightened.

The experience Muldoon had at age 21 evokes additional questions, similar to the story of Mrs. B. Do people who experience astral travel aim in some inexplicable way to meet particular people who can see them / identify with their state / experience similar states of consciousness? What creates the contact between people who have this experience spontaneously? Does the fact that a person who is familiar with the out-of-body experience has the ability to accept and understand make the astral visit of another person in his life possible? Does the ability for openness and extrasensory reception (that sometimes stems from a particular physical and mental state – such as the case of old Mrs. M.) help in the encounter between the astral traveler and the person who can feel his presence or see him? And like the amazing case of Ed Morrell, who met his future wife during astral travel – is there such a thing as a "guiding hand" or an unconscious ability of the "upper I" to guide the astral traveler to a place where there is someone he has to meet?

This special case occurred in the summer of 1924, when Muldoon lived alone in a small town near Wisconsin. One warm evening, Muldoon was eating a late dinner alone in the cabin where he lived. He was feeling low, and he decided to go out for a short stroll before going to sleep. The weather was pleasant and relatively warm, and the full moon illuminated the path. Muldoon walked slowly along the paths near his house, hoping that the pleasant weather and the moonlight would cheer him up. After walking for a while without the slightest improvement in his mood, he returned home gloomily. He locked the door and went back to bed. Just as he was beginning to doze off, he felt his body float up into the air and pass through doors and walls. In a few moments he was outside. He began to be swept and pulled uncontrollably, but not in such a threatening way as during his first experience. Within a short time he found himself in the living-room of a strange and unfamiliar house. He looked around. There were four people in the room, but one of them – a pretty girl of about 17 – attracted his attention. He stood opposite her and looked at her, momentarily hypnotized by the movements of her fingers that were embroidering white lace for a sleek black velvet dress. After a few minutes, he resumed floating in the room and examined the furniture and objects carefully. After that, he left the house and returned to his room.

He etched the trip in his memory, and went on with his life as usual, trying to invest all of his energy in his college studies. Two weeks after the incident, when he was walking home from college, a familiar movement not far away attracted his attention. He approached, and saw the same girl he had encountered during his journey going into the house of one of his neighbors. The door closed behind her, and he decided to wait for her to come out. When she came out of the neighbor's house, Muldoon was waiting for her at the fence. She passed by him, and he hurried after her. Since he knew that she did not live in the area, he asked her without hesitation where she lived. The girl was astonished at the audacity of young stranger's question. In those days, it was plain rude to go up to a girl you didn't know and ask her such a personal question.

Illustrations from Muldoon and Carrington's book –
Spotlight on the Astral Body.

Muldoon tried to calm her down – and actually did so when he began to describe her house very accurately. He recalled the heavy furniture in the living-room, the way it was arranged, the few ornaments and even the odd pictures hanging on the wall. Surprisingly, the girl's astonishment waned and she was silent for a few moments, looking at him with such interest that Muldoon succumbed to the temptation of telling her how he knew all these details. To his surprise, the girl did not express any skepticism about his special experience, and told him that she herself had had similar astral journeys! They became close friends, and could share their special experiences freely and openly.

Muldoon's out-of-body experiences occurred fairly frequently throughout his life. The wonderful experience of meeting people astrally without them seeing him near them and afterwards actually meeting up with those same people also recurred throughout his life. He began to take a greater and greater interest in astral travel, and began to investigate the phenomenon. One of his hypotheses regarding the origin of the phenomenon was that the underlying reason for out-of-body experiences was a serious physical illness or an emotional shock that changed the person's physical balance, and the astral body was a kind of cosmic energy that emanated from the body and continued to move and travel to different places.

One of the famous "astral travelers" is Robert Monroe, who transformed the out-of-body experiences into an art, researched it in depth, invented a popular method for doing it, and even established an institute for brain research and astral experiences in Virginia. Because of his great importance in this field, I will briefly present his biography.

Robert Allen Monroe was born in Lexington, Kentucky, to a mother who was a physician and a father who was a university professor. He began his studies at elementary school at age four, and completed his academic studies at the University of Ohio, where he studied paramedical engineering, arts and sciences. Upon graduating in 1937, he began to work as a writer and producer in radio stations in Cleveland and Cincinatti.

In 1939, Monroe moved to New York, where he wrote and produced his first program for the "Rocky Gordon" radio networks. After he had worked as a producer and the manager of a radiophonic advertising agency for a time, he established a company called RAM, which produced radio programs up until 1956. At that time, Monroe's company was producing some of the most successful contemporary radio programs. Monroe's reputation spread far and wide and he became a kind of celebrity, and in parallel began to publish personal columns in the press. Monroe, who was blessed with multiple talents, did not make do with producing radio programs and writing in the newspaper. He began to compose music for the radio, the cinema, and for TV programs.

With the expansion of Monroe's company into other states in the US, the name of his company was changed to "Monroe Industries" in 1956, and the company began to engage in the development and installation of cable television.

Monroe's interest in human consciousness began in 1956, when he initiated a small research project for developing programs for the New York branch of his company. The aim of the research was to check out the possibility of learning while sleeping. In 1958, key data were found – an almost unknown state of consciousness, differentiated from and different than the physical body. The group of researchers coined the name "Out-of-Body Experience" (OBE) as the scientific definition for astral travel. Today, this concept is used by scientists and researchers who are interested in exploring astral travel. In the years following, Monroe and his group of researchers began to work on means and methods to invoke and control this ability, at the same time conducting studies on additional states of consciousness in their research laboratories. All of Monroe's researchers, and Monroe himself, were considered to be unique experts in creating effective sound patterns as part of their work in radio and TV research, and of Monroe's personal and professional affinity to the sound processed in electronic instruments. They used these abilities as a basis for their research. Their efforts ultimately produced clear and significant results scientifically, sparking international interest. Scientists, physicians, psychologists, physicists, psychiatrists, research engineers and even non-professional people began to take an interest in the results of the studies of Monroe and his group. Monroe took out three patents in his name dealing the reception and entry into various states of consciousness, and they become known throughout the world. After Monroe's magic touch, the idea of astral travel turned from an abstract mystical idea to a fascinating and viable scientific topic. In 1973, the "Monroe Institute" was established by the original nucleus of the group of researchers and began to hold study seminars meant both for the general public and for professional people in various fields whose interest was the ability to control human states of consciousness. The seminars were held in several places inside the United States as well as outside of the country. Nowadays, the research and studies are held mainly at the Monroe Institute in Virginia, which, besides auditoriums and seminar rooms, also contains research labs and recording studios. The research activities of the Monroe Institute created a new popular-scientific facet in the attitude toward astral travel – toward the out-of-body experience and toward understanding different states of consciousness, and toward the control and use of the abilities of the human brain. In 1971, Monroe's book, Journeys Outside of the Body, was published.

The course of Monroe's life and the chronology of his professional success are very interesting in relation to his abilities to embark on astral travel. If we look at his life, it seems that his entire professional path, from the beginning, led him to developing and making the general public aware of the various states of consciousness. His *modus operandi* is the dream of every creator and scientist.

On the one hand, it consisted of in-depth research, with a holistic ability to see the different functions that could help in the development of the research, as well as creative and unique thinking that combined art, medicine, science and awareness into a single whole.

On the other, it demonstrated the ability not only to make his research topic popular with, understood by and interesting to the general public, but also to stimulate the curiosity of the scientific community. Monroe's success-filled life and self-realization inspire the question: Did some kind of guiding hand guide young Monroe's steps? Did the creative and far-reaching information that formed in his brain gain the continuous and directing support of the universe?

Monroe's becoming a successful TV producer and one of the first people to support cable TV (which afforded him tremendous financial resources for the continuation of his scientific-creative-spiritual activities) is not mere coincidence. Thirty years before the invention of television, when he was still a child, Monroe predicted the television era and its undoubted influence on human awareness.

Monroe's astral journeys did not begin at one magical moment. They were gradual and filled with distinct unpleasantness. In an attempt to pinpoint the moment when Monroe experienced the beginning of his expanded consciousness, we can mention the day in his youth when he lay on his bed and began to feel agonizing cramps and convulsions in his entire body. Lying in pain on his bed,

Monroe let his arm slip down and hang loosely next to the bed.

Suddenly, he felt his fingers passing through the carpet. He pushed his arm, and his whole arm went through the floor without any resistance from the solid matter! Many years later, Monroe said that he had no doubt that he was completely awake at the time. As he grew up, the attacks of pain and cramps became stronger and stronger. In one incident, when he was already a young married man, the pain was so intense and out of control that he fell on the floor. As he fell, he felt that he was going through the floor, and the sensation of intense pain changed into a feeling of light floating, like a balloon drifting in the air.

Suddenly, the feeling of lightness changed into astonishment and rage – he saw his wife lying in their double bed with a man. He scrutinized the man who was sleeping peacefully in the bed – and identified himself. At that moment, he tried to return to his physical body, and succeeded in doing so easily. He woke up in his bed next to his wife, who was fast asleep.

In contrast to Muldoon and Ed Morrell, Monroe did not visit only known places on earth in the present, but also other dimensions, which he called "realities" – reality A, reality B, and reality C.

The first reality is the reality of the world in which we live in the present.

The second reality is the world of thought, the mental world, which Monroe considered to be the natural environment of the astral body. In the second reality, Monroe saw what people are inclined to define as "heaven and hell," and there he met the spirits of people who no longer lived in the first reality.

The third reality Monroe visited was the reality of a world similar to ours, but its technological level and several of its properties were different from those that we know. In that reality, Monroe met people who looked like people who were in the first reality (our world, as it is here and now), visited cities and saw roads and buildings that were similar to those that exist in the reality that is familiar to us. However, the customs of the people in this reality were different, and it was based on a technology that was different than ours. For instance, in that realty, the use of gasoline did not exist, and it even looked as if the development of science in that reality was less advanced, or different than what we know. But Monroe would go out to visit this reality, adopting his other, astral body, which was a "physical body" in the dimensions of that reality, and live a different life than the life experienced in the reality that is known to us.

Today, the idea of different "realities," different dimensions, is no longer only the province of science fiction, but a possibility that is being seriously studied by several research bodies in the world of physics and science.

Tools for spiritual work

Improving extrasensory abilities

Some people think that only special types are endowed with supernatural abilities, and that these abilities are innate, a cosmic gift granted to exceptional individuals only. In truth, however, we all have various supernatural abilities, and the sixth sense is not only the gift of exceptional people, but is accessible to each one of us. An in-depth look at everyday life is likely to reveal how we use our sixth sense, sometimes incidentally. Those times the phone rings, and you know exactly who is at the other end of the line, are not at all rare. Similarly, there is the widespread experience of thinking of someone – remembering him suddenly – and shortly afterwards receiving a letter or an unexpected call from him.

Telepathy is an "extrasensory" sense that has been satisfactorily preserved in many people. I have known many people who did not use any of their extrasensory senses for a long time, but after they began to develop their awareness and their extrasensory abilities, they managed to discover extrasensory talents within them relatively easily. Each one of us is able to develop the extrasensory senses that are within us – inside the code of our soul – and are not something external. To this day, in my experience, anyone who truly began to live a more aware life and make an effort to develop his awareness and his extrasensory abilities, developed one or more of his extrasensory abilities fully.

Of course, there are people who find it easier than others to develop their extrasensory abilities. Some of them have a natural ability that was not repressed during childhood, and was allowed to develop naturally. Some are people who engaged in profound work on their awareness, sometimes without any conscious effort, but rather because of a need that sprang from a difficult life – a situation that compelled them "to take themselves in hand" and peer into the depths of their soul. By gazing into the depths of their soul, by learning to balance the unharmonious ones, their extrasensory abilities also begin to reveal themselves gradually and naturally.

Because of what we have read in books and seen in movies and on TV, there is a general belief that extrasensory abilities are "mediumistic abilities" that "land" on the person from out of the blue and cause him to become a mouthpiece for the spirits or to switch the chips so that he wins a fortune in a casino, and so forth. In fact, it is true extrasensory ability that helps him know intuitively what is right or not right for him, discover and recognize his vocation in life, and have the ability – that cannot be explained "logically" – to turn his life into an ideal existence filled with the satisfaction and self-realization he dreamed of.

The purpose of the extrasensory abilities that each one of us possesses is not to perform flashy wonders in front of capacity audiences, to exorcise demons, or to solve murder cases by holding an object that belonged to the victim. Of course, those abilities have their place in the world, but they are the objective of the people who are destined to demonstrate them, and not everyone's aim in life is to be Uri Geller. In contrast, everyone has the obligation to be a healer – his own healer, the healer of his body, mind, and spirit – so that he can repair his life in this incarnation and realize his vocation. This vocation can be anything you can think of, from being an activist in an environmental movement to establishing and developing a happy and harmonious domestic life.

To this end, the first step toward using extrasensory abilities, which are an absolutely natural part of the code of our soul, is also the first step leading to their natural development. These two parameters support each other in a perfect circular manner. It is the step toward discovering our vocation, repairing our lives, and realizing ourselves.

The mental processes that the person has to undergo in order to realize his physical, mental, and spiritual potential are the same processes that lead to spiritual enlightenment. The extrasensory abilities that are revealed in the person as he follows the path of his soul in order to realize his vocation differ greatly from person to person. Sometimes, they will not be as "glamorous" as Uri Geller's abilities, for instance, part of whose vocation in the world was to let people see the spiritual potential that exists in them. However, they are specific abilities that support the person while he realizes his vocation in life.

As an example, we can examine the various talents with which people are endowed, and see how extrasensory abilities support them.

If part of a person's vocation in life is to be a writer, for instance, he may discover that when his extrasensory abilities develop, they make him strongly "intuitive," able to receive intuitive messages that turn his written creation into something significant, both for the repair of his soul and for the benefit of mankind. He may, for example, discover channeling abilities, automatic writing abilities, and so on. A person who discovers that his soul yearns to paint may discover that meditative painting, or "channeled creation," is developing in him. Concomitantly, the emphasis is being placed on two crucial things in his life: developing his extrasensory abilities (from which it is not possible to separate the work on the awareness of body, mind, and spirit), and following his path of destiny – investing his energy in his creative talent. A person whose vocation in life is to build a warm and loving family unit, thus increasing mental and spiritual health in the world, and to go on increasing the critical mass of true maternal-paternal and conjugal love, may discover, for instance, that his abilities to be naturally empathetichave become very strong, because they will support the realization of his vocation. A person whose function is to raise the world's consciousness about the plight of animals, for instance, may well discover, upon developing his extrasensory abilities and his spiritual awareness, that he can channel with animals easily and naturally. (Consciousness-raising does not necessarily mean making speeches in the United Nations, but rather increasing the critical mass of people who are aware of a certain matter by adding "one soul", that of the particular person, to the general awareness of the subject.) And so on.

In other words, our extrasensory abilities are not separate from our entity and our aim in life. They constitute an inseparable part of the realization of our vocation in the world. Similarly, it is impossible to separate the development of the extrasensory ability from the work on balancing mind and body, because only a well-balanced body, mind, and spirit can make correct and superior use of the extrasensory abilities. There are people who do not work on their soul in depth, and instead permit it to be an inhibiting factor (by constantly harboring anger, sadness, negative beliefs in life, and so on). When these people are gifted with extrasensory abilities, they are liable to cause a great deal of damage to themselves and to the world because they are unable to channel their energies correctly. As an example, we can look at the conduct of various mediums who are indeed gifted with a powerful extrasensory ability, but since they exploit it to inflate their ego, they have to create an illusion in which it is far more powerful or eccentric than it really is. They fall into the trap that they themselves have set in order to continue inflating their ego with "I am the great, powerful medium who can make ghosts appear in front of people's eyes." Of course, the damage that is caused to people, to the spiritual awareness in the world, and to the medium himself is enormous.

For this reason, before beginning to develop your extrasensory talents, you must stop and think: What is my aim in developing them? What do I expect to get out of the fact that they are stronger? Do I intend to use them to increase and deepen my spiritual awareness, or to bolster and inflate my unbalanced ego? Will I use them as a helpful tool for discovering my vocation in life and as a support for finding the various ways of repairing my soul and realizing my vocation, or will I use them for creating devious means of achieving aims that do not in the least resemble my basic and vocational aim?

Finding one's vocation in life

This is undoubtedly an eye-catching title. Who doesn't want to find his vocation in life? We all hope to go to sleep at night and wake up in the morning saying, "That's it! That's my vocation in life. Now I know."

That is certainly possible, but it does not always happen that way. The path to finding our vocation in life pauses at an extremely important point – the **desire** to find our vocation in life.

This involves taking personal responsibility for our lives (and that is a serious matter – understanding that we create the reality of our lives, and no longer blaming other people or the universe for things that happen in our lives) and the decision to seek and find the path along which we were meant to realize our existence in this world. The development and use of extrasensory abilities can be extremely powerful in helping us find our vocation in life. However, these insights may not come to us overnight, either, but rather little by little, step by step, just like the realization of our vocation itself occurs in little steps, and not in one day. Even if the person discovers that his vocation in life is to establish a harmonious and love-filled family life, the discovery of his vocation will not lead to his being married and father of three within a week, with no obstacle or deep spiritual work along his path. Having said this, the fact that he has this information will throw open the gates to realizing his vocation. Fortunate people, whose desire to discover their vocation in life is very strong and directs their entire lifestyle, are likely to be successful in this within a few years – if they invest all their energy in the search. Ultimately, however, time is not very significant to them, since what are a few years as compared to the eternity of our souls?

In contrast, developing extrasensory abilities helps us at the various stages of the path to finding our vocation and realizing it. It also helps develop the mental and spiritual harmony we need for the rest of the path. The ways of helping are many and varied, and the fact of being aware of them, and afterwards using them, will lead to far-reaching changes in life. Here are a few examples:

Dreaming: Through dreaming, we can receive messages about the situation in life we are in at the moment, about the path we are following, and about the path our soul wishes to follow (these two are not always the same!). Indeed, when the person knows how to make the correct use of dreams, he can really get up one morning and know what his vocation in life is. This must be preceded by a true and sincere desire to discover the path, and a deep commitment to follow it. Even if such an extreme change does not occur, awareness is likely to come gradually by means of in-depth dream work.

Channeling, meditation with crystals, meditation to discover previous incarnations: By knowing our soul's past, we can understand our present and receive clues about the "future." The development of channeling abilities and work with crystals as an excellent tool for increasing self-awareness and spiritual awareness will provide us with additional pieces for understanding this puzzle, which is the sum total that constitutes the "I." When we discover one of our incarnations, we can understand why our soul has chosen to undergo certain kinds of experiences in our present incarnation. We can understand some of the components and properties of our personality, as well as the nature of some of the "obstacles" and "inhibitions" that face us in life. Working with crystals and stones helps in as many ways as there are crystals and stones, starting with the ability to discover previous incarnations, and ending with the raising/dissolving of emotional and mental patterns, among them the various traumas from this life and from previous incarnations.

Telepathy, energy-sensing abilities, and awareness of inner and outer energies: When telepathy and the various ways of intuitively picking up energies and their significance reach a level at which the person can "sense" the thoughts, intentions, and emotions of another person, they are extremely powerful tools when the person knows how to use them. People who are gifted with a powerful telepathic ability or a high level of energetic sensitivity, occasionally tend to complain. They say, "Just imagine. I walk into a room and I immediately sense what this one or that one is feeling. Those emotions/intentions/thoughts are not always pleasant! Sometimes it makes me want to simply get up and run out of there, away from those people!"

In that example, it is possible to see how the extent of mental and spiritual work the person has done on himself is expressed in his ability to make effective use of the extrasensory ability itself. When this ability comes to the person without a profound insight of the basic laws of the universe, it is liable to seem like a nuisance, and not as a supportive ability. In contrast, when the person has assimilated the laws of the universe properly and lives accordingly, he knows that every person, feeling, emotion, and even energy that is brought to his attention actually serves as a self-mirror that shows him which aspects of his personality are still not balanced. Therefore, when he senses a pattern of rage in a certain person, for example, he will immediately look inside himself to see how that pattern is embodied in his personality. When he is able to do that, he receives an ongoing status report of what repair he himself needs, as if he were in a workshop for developing and balancing the soul hour after hour. After he has found the inner pattern inside himself, he can pay attention to it and begin mental and spiritual work to understand this pattern in his soul, and thus work toward balancing it.

Of course, the ability to balance and repair mental patterns in our personality is invaluable, and is one of the strongest and most genuine ways of attaining spiritual depth and even spiritual enlightenment. The latter are expressed in every aspect of our life; they help us recognize our vocation in life, and assist us along the long path toward realizing it.

There are endless examples – the above are only a tiny fraction. However, to sum up the influence of the extrasensory abilities on the path we follow in order to know ourselves in depth and realize our vocation in life, it can be said that their most significant effect is the ability to understand profoundly and truly the way the world works, and the truth behind the material illusion in which we live. When the person is enlightened by the insight that life in this world is actually a temporary illusion, and nothing that seems to us to be "vital," or an "insurmountable obstacle" is "genuine" or cannot be changed in some way, he is halfway to the discovery and realization of his vocation in life. After this comprehension, the obstacles that people tend to put up for themselves suddenly seem like just an illusion, which, by means of conscious work, will, and effort, can be removed and discarded. (Every person puts up obstacles that block his path to the discovery and realization of his vocation: "I don't have money," "My wife is holding me back," "I don't have time," "It's too difficult/not possible," "I'm not good /clever enough" "I'm too old/fat/tall/short," etc.) The understanding provided by the extrasensory ability – being able to activate abilities that are "beyond nature" (referring to what we were taught about the meaning of "nature" and "natural" at school…) – causes the person to understand that life is much deeper than what it seems on the surface, and that his abilities in every field are much greater than what they seem. No less important is that the person learns in this way to recognize that what he sees with his physical eyes and experiences with his physical senses is not "everything that exists and no more." He learns to understand that there are reasons for things, and even things that can drive him crazy at times are important and contribute to his life. Of course, life with this kind of awareness quickly becomes easier, because a lot of the things that succeeded in eroding our strength and our belief in ourselves are shattered in the face of a strong basic personality and awareness.

A warning about the use of extrasensory abilities

It is important to point out that your mental state and rational ability to accept or reject exceptional phenomena exert an enormous influence on your ability to increase your extrasensory abilities. However, there is no doubt that with practice, awareness, and confidence, you can increase your abilities. How you use these abilities is your business, but a warning about this is in order. In general, attempts to influence various people to do something that is not right, appropriate for them, or moral, are not successful. Every attempt to misuse extrasensory powers carries a personal price that is sometimes a heavy one.

An interesting thing that happened to me illustrates how "pulling the string too tight" is liable to cause problems. This type of "pulling the string" mainly stems from some kind of personality trait that is not sufficiently balanced, and tempts the person to use his extrasensory abilities in a way that is not absolutely pure. I became aware that by means of the power of thought, I could "invite" certain events into my life. So, often before leaving on a trip, or sometimes even before going out, I would focus my thoughts on the desire to meet someone who could provide me with information on certain things I was involved with, channel with me about a certain topic, or shed light on a topic that I had not understood sufficiently. Over the years, this ability developed and became stronger, until I could declare, before going to a particular place, "Today I'll meet a person who knows a lot about building sets for movies." And indeed, completely "coincidentally," I would land up meeting a person who was knowledgeable about precisely the subject I was interested in. Having said that, I would always start off by requesting the consent and support of the universe, knowing that we are not allowed to use our powers for obtaining things that are not to the universal force's "liking." Once, when I tried to use this power incorrectly, I was taught not to do so again:

Several years ago, I saw a movie on TV. One of the characters reminded me of a person I had not seen since high school.

That boy was an exceptionally talented actor, and out of some kind of egoistic desire, I decided that I wanted to meet him then and there so that he could teach me a few acting techniques that could help me develop my acting ability. I did not have a good feeling about this wish; I felt as if I was trying to change the order of the universe with it, and that the person had no desire to meet me at that time. Despite that, I insisted. I knew that our whole group of friends was supposed to go out to some place I had never been to, and I decided that that would be a good place to meet that guy. I used my powers to invite him to the place and create a reality in which I would meet him there. As opposed to previous times, I did not simply request to meet a person who would help me with a particular matter, but I insisted on meeting that specific person. Obstinately, out of excessive pride ("It always works for me..."), I went on creating the specific reality. I got all dressed up for the evening, and exchanged my eyeglasses for contact lenses so as to put the finishing touches to my appearance.

During the journey, while I was still busy ordering the

event, I began to feel discomfort in one eye. Within a short time, the feeling turned into a sharp, penetrating pain, and I realized that one of the lenses had slipped off my pupil. Not pleasant, perhaps, but not terrible. Generally, you can take out the lens and stop the painful sensation easily. Not this time, however. We stopped at a gas station, and I tried to extract the lens – to no avail. I did not manage to extract it or to relocate it over my pupil, and the pain became more and more severe. I have used lenses for many years, but I have never experienced that kind of pain, and so extreme. By the time we reached the city, it was unbearable. My eye was red and swollen, burning and watering, and the pain was piercing and incessant. I have to admit that I even became slightly hysterical because of the severe pain. Concerned, my friends quickly stopped the car in the city center so that I could go into a restaurant and look at my eye in a mirror in a well-lit place. We passed three or four places, and then we came to a pizzeria in which there was a well-lit bathroom. I climbed the stairs to the bathroom and tried to extract the lens. It was almost impossible. I began to cry angrily from pain and frustration. The outing was supposed to be cool and fun, and here I was, being a drag, stuck with a lens that was killing me!

Help came from an unexpected quarter: One of the pizzeria workers, whose entrance I hadn't noticed because I was so stressed out, came upstairs to the floor where the bathrooms were and began to explain what I should do to get the lens out. When I eventually managed to extract it according to his instructions, I washed my face and calmed down a bit. Then I turned to thank the guy. To my surprise, he resembled the guy I had used my powers to meet like two peas in a pod – except for one difference: that guy had red hair, while this one had black hair. Except for that single difference, they were so similar that I immediately understood what was going on – my inflated ego had blinded my eyes to taking the laws of the universe into account. I could have dubbed this event a "coincidence" had I not been given clear intuitive knowledge of what was going to happen before we went out (a feeling about the future that is about to happen, as if in the "past," a second of seeing future events). Even so, I stubbornly ignored the knowledge I had received.

Although this is a "small" example, I learned from a great deal of experience in the use of thought energy for creating various realities that when we try to "impose" our will on reality, knowing deep inside that it is neither right or proper, we are liable to experience some kind of event that will teach us not to do it again. Over the years, it happened that I met a number of people who had abused their powers in order to get other people to do what they wanted them to do. I got away from them as quickly as possible, since their energetic proximity is not healthy. However, when I met all those people several years later, every one of them was suffering from some serious problem or other – physical or mental, as I had intuitively supposed would happen to them if they continued using their powers negatively. Therefore, even when we succeed in developing our extrasensory abilities, it is very important to notice how we use them and to listen to the inner feelings that tell us if a certain use of the powers is wrong or not in line with the will of the universe. Any attempt to impose our will on someone else or to cause a natural occurrence to veer from its course exacts a certain price, either then and there or at a later date.

Developing the extrasensory abilities how do we "do" it?

A common question regarding extrasensory abilities is: "How do I do it? How do I develop those abilities by myself?"

Frankly, there is no simple answer. There is no single way, method, or technique that will make you clairvoyant, telepathic, or able to see auras or visions from one day to the next.

Having extrasensory abilities is more a way of life than a talent. This ability depends more on our perception of the world, on the way we relate to our world and communicate with it, than on study, technique, or a set of laws.

Having said that, there are ways to acquire the ability. There are laws, there are techniques – but even then, this ability is the embodiment of the force of the soul inside you, and as such, the whole is greater than its parts.

Certain cosmic laws and principles are true laws felt by every person who is linked to his soul and channels, regardless of what his religion is, which culture he belongs to, or which tools he uses to arouse his extrasensory ability. It is no coincidence that those are exactly the same laws for a holistic and aware life.

In order for the person to be able to realize his full potential, to fulfill his abilities and discover his paths to the world beyond the senses, he must be able to learn to see, feel, and live himself and the world around him holistically.

Learning the cosmic laws and principles will help you

not only develop your extrasensory talents, but derive tremendous enjoyment from all strata of life. They will expand and deepen your everyday life, and through them you can discover new insights of your own. When these laws are familiar to you, the insights and messages that await you will arrive.

Development of extrasensory abilities

The judgment obstacle

When judgment is not objective, it is liable to be one of the main "enemies" of the extrasensory ability. When I say "judgment," I mean everything you have learned and accumulated over the years – the large amount of information that has been internalized, a great deal of which consists of prejudices, subjective suppositions, superstitions, and so on. Judgment can be a wonderful tool for helping a person who has supernatural powers, but only when he knows how to recognize the basic prejudices that exist in him.

Judgment stems from what we have learned about this world via our senses, at home, in our community. Prejudice regarding extrasensory activity that claims – consciously or unconsciously, and sometimes in a profound and hidden manner – that any experience of this type is impossible, nonsensical, and unscientific, has been shown by researchers to exert a significant influence on the ability to experience extrasensory phenomena. It can also prevent an extrasensory phenomenon that the person experienced spontaneously from being repeated.

The effect of prejudice on the extrasensory ability has been clearly demonstrated in two famous sets of studies. The first is the renowned study known as "The 'Sheep-Goat' Effect," and the second is a multiple-subject study on telekinesis.

The study known as "The 'Sheep-Goat' Effect" was conducted in 1942 by the professor of psychology, Gertrude Schmeidler, from New York University. She devised a questionnaire in order to examine students' beliefs and prejudices regarding extrasensory activity. She used the term "sheep" to indicate the students who were sure of the existence of extrasensory occurrences, and "goats" for those who were skeptical about the possibility of the existence of extrasensory activity in general, as it was presented in the questionnaire. After the questionnaires had been checked, she gave the subjects a classic test of extrasensory abilities, after which they were given a classic test of telepathic abilities and clairvoyant abilities. This was done by means of special cards, where the subjects had to guess card sequences.

Schmeidler compared the results of the questionnaires with those of the extrasensory tests, and the astounding facts showed that in the "sheep" group, there was a far above average deviation toward positive results in the extrasensory and the telepathic-clairvoyant tests, while the results of the "goat" group demonstrated a significant deviation below the curve of the usual chance of success in this type of test.

Following this study, many other studies were performed, some of them in recent years, clearly demonstrating the systematic accumulation of wrong answers in people who do not believe in extrasensory abilities, as opposed to a high proportion of correct answers in tests done by people who believed in them. The studies conclude that people who believe in the existence of extrasensory phenomena systematically achieve an above-average number of correct answers, while the achievement of the "non-believers" is systematically below average. Studies performed with the specific purpose of examining this phenomenon demonstrated that certain individuals are able to reach such a high level of "wrong answers" that this itself is a kind of "extrasensory phenomenon" no less than the above-average ability to guess the correct cards – showing that this is not a matter of poor extrasensory ability in the "goats." On the contrary, it would seem that these people unconsciously use their extrasensory powers to evade the aim of the test, and unconsciously sabotage their results!

We tend to select information that confirms our beliefs and ignore information that is not compatible with them. Selective perception plays an important role in the personal interpretation of what seem to be extrasensory experiences. Skeptics tend to declare that people who believe in extrasensory phenomena are inclined to see "extrasensory phenomena" in everything, even up to the point of confusing their personal interpretations with the real events. In contrast, non-believers tend to refute situations that seem to be extrasensory experiences, and find "rational" reasons for explaining extrasensory experiences, even when they occur in their lives. But the sheep-goat effect shows that this goes beyond the individual's personal interpretation – the attitude of the person toward extrasensory phenomena influences the probability that phenomena of this type will occur at all. The more the person fosters a narrow view of the world, so his chances of such phenomena occurring in his life decrease. The more interested the person is in a holistic view of the world, and the more open to extrasensory experiences he is, the greater the chances are that the universe will "react" to this by creating experiences of this type.

The second set of tests that stressed this principle focused even more on the practical ability of the subjects to repeat an extrasensory activity after an initial incidence of success. In the set of studies that included large groups of people (between 60 and 100), more than 70% of the subjects succeeded, to varying extents and by means of the correct guidance, in using the power of thought to bend metal. Fewer than 30% succeeded in repeating the experiment a second time. After in-depth research, the reason for this phenomenon emerged: after the person succeeded in bending the metal clearly and surprisingly, he experienced a reaction of being unable to explain the phenomena scientifically, and this created an intellectual paradox that prevented him from being able to repeat the phenomenon.

In order to be able to pick up clear, authentic, and clean extrasensory messages, without causing yourself uneasy feelings, you will have to learn how to distance the sometimes almost automatic subjective judgment that springs up in you upon seeing various visions or messages. Your personal opinions, tendencies, past experiences and background are liable to affect both the manner in which you receive the messages and how you decipher and understand them. The greater your ability to accept matters with great openness, without activating your "automatic" judgment and expressing your personal opinion, the broader and more surprising the range of messages that reach you will be. At the same time, along with the activity to improve and develop your intuition, you will begin to discover your prejudices, fears, and subjective opinions and beliefs, and you will know how to neutralize them when they do not support you and your intuitive activities.

The obstacle of fear

The obstacle of fear is extremely powerful. If we nourish it energetically, it is liable to completely thwart our attempts to experience our extrasensory abilities. The fear can be a mixture of prejudices, guilt feelings, or even the feeling of "doing something bad" regarding dabbling in the world beyond the senses. You should ask yourself the following questions in order to dispel fears and uncomfortable feelings, most of which are unconscious, about dealing with the extrasensory:

Was anyone in your family, or in your close surroundings – especially when you were a child – deeply afraid of any contact with the extrasensory world? Did adults in your surroundings tend, for any reason, to define this practice as "satanic" or "dangerous"? Is supernatural activity linked with "madness" or "insanity" in any part of your consciousness? Did anyone in your close surroundings, or when you were a child, practice black magic (and was hurt at some stage or other)? Does anyone in your close surroundings tend to relate to extrasensory activity as "nonsense"? Were your brought up to believe that "it's forbidden to dabble in those things"?

We live in the world of beliefs that we create. Prejudices play a very powerful part in the formation of our worldview, and our worldview is one of our tools for forming reality, most certainly in the extrasensory world. Fear and anxiety following any extrasensory experience (even a very positive one), resulting from a belief that the world of extrasensory phenomena is dangerous or unclean, are liable to cause a number of phenomena:

1. Inability to repeat the extrasensory experience you had, because of "panic" and surprise at the very fact of your success and what was revealed to you.

2. Soliciting frightening experiences from the extrasensory realm, and increased sensitivity to non-positive energy, vulnerability and sensitivity that stem from a weak aura because of psychological fear, which is liable to cause nightmares, fear of entities, and so on.

3. Linking extrasensory activity with madness is liable to make you unable to channel the extrasensory messages you receive – again, because of anxiety or a paralyzing fear that interferes with the improvement and increase in your extrasensory powers, and because of the unconscious or conscious fear that these things are liable to cause you to lose your mind.

Fanatic religious faith

Fanatic religious faith, especially the kind that originates in the home, constitutes a very powerful obstacle for many people who experiment with extrasensory phenomena, and makes them anxious about their achievements. This is generally because certain religious groups link extrasensory activities with satanism, idolatory, and so on. The majority of these links are completely baseless. It must be remembered that the religious writings in the various cultures are full of miraculous deeds and extrasensory phenomena! In both the Old and New Testaments, many of the prophets and other figures were gifted with these powers and used them. It was precisely those extrasensory abilities, such as prophetic ability, clairvoyance, channeling, healing by touch, and so on, that turned "religious heroes" into lofty and holy spiritual figures. If this is the case, why do various religious currents deny the existence of extrasensory phenomena and make people fear them? After all, extrasensory abilities, when they are developed, channeled, and used correctly, help the person distinguish between right and wrong, and help him attain a close and direct relationship with his soul. Of course, this would render all these preachers worthless, and is liable to undermine various religious structures whose source lies in the desire to control, and not in the desire to lead people to love God.

In contrast, various spiritual occupations may very well be dangerous – a large percentage of those involved in them come to harm. This has been proved. Among these occupations, we can include all fields of black magic, voodoo, raising the spirits of the dead, and seances.

However, these things are not dangerous because the rabbi, the priest, or Mom said so. They are dangerous because they constitute a distorted use of extrasensory powers, which, according to the laws of the universe, is accompanied by pain and suffering, just like insisting on touching a hot iron turns an ostensibly innocent appliance into one that is dangerous and threatening. I sincerely recommend that you not try things of this type because I have seen many dire consequences as well as the energetic distortion they cause. In contrast, when a person heals by means of energies, prior information, prophecy, feeling auras, and so on, and does so with a pure heart, a good intention, and love, he will attract the same kind of energies as he is sending to the cosmos – healing energies, love, and understanding.

Religious faith is liable to create an additional problem when the person attributes information, insights, or messages to a certain figure (among many Christians, it is common to attribute all healing powers to Jesus – even when this is not the case), and this interferes with his objective scrutiny of his abilities. It is not a good idea to "decide" that the powers with which you are blessed derive from a particular religious source, when this is not the case – it is just your subjective impression.

Coping with fear

It is important to know that every extrasensory experience becomes more powerful if you are afraid of it. Even if the experience is not pleasant, even if you feel a great deal of discomfort, ask yourself: "Can this really hurt me?" It cannot really hurt you unless you really, really want it to…

Negative entities are attracted to fear and terror. The more frightened attention you pay them, the stronger they will seem to you to become. The more you try to flee, the more it will seem to you that they are becoming stronger. When you stop fleeing, they will lose interest in you. Sometimes, certain experiences are liable to be frightening, and you will find that it is not easy to feel confident. Accept your fear, and don't fight it, but don't cling to it either. If you try to fight fear, you may be trying to control an emotion that cannot be controlled at that moment, and you will only stress yourself out more. What you can do in such cases is *to choose not to cling to fear*. Acknowledge your fears and accept them, but remember that any extrasensory attack is extrasensory, that is, it is not physical, and cannot really hurt you. An experience of this kind can hurt by causing fear and anxiety. When you recall this, the fear will pass more quickly, and you can apply suitable techniques for dispelling an extrasensory attack or non-positive energy. Similarly, developing emotions of humility, understanding, and compassion toward those entities, or toward people who emit negative energy, will help you dissipate disturbances of this type very quickly.

Work on the "self"

Work on the "self" is the first and most important tool for discovering the extrasensory abilities that exist in us. These abilities do not come to us from the outside; they already exist within us, and we have to discover them. When we cleanse ourselves of all those numerous layers that hold us back and prevent us from discovering the full potential that exists in us, this potential will begin to realize itself naturally.

Old input – get out, new input, come in!

Work with inhibiting thought patterns

This is one of many exercises that serve to reveal negative thought patterns and get rid of them by replacing them with new and supportive thought "input." This exercise comes in many variations, and you yourself may well discover the variation that suits you the most. In order to illustrate how to work, I will use a simple example that demonstrates the influence of the mental layer on the physical layer – sore feet.

You are advised to do the exercise on paper, with the date.

First stage: **The problem**

At the first stage, let's address one problem or issue in life that is bothering us. This problem may be physical or emotional, connected with a relationship, with our income, with creativity – or anything else that belongs to our personal world.

Issues we define as "problems" are a very powerful tool for our spiritual development, even though we sometimes tend to moan about them. As Richard Bach wrote in his book, "Illusions": "There is no such thing as a problem that is not presenting you with a gift. You seek problems because you need their gifts." In this exercise, we will isolate one problem and try to discover its gift of awareness to us. The problem I have chosen is sore feet.

Second stage: **What does the problem represent for me?**

At this stage, we will divide the verbal definition of the problem up into factors, and we will try to understand what the essence of the matter symbolizes for us. In the example I have chosen, the question, "What is pain *for me?*", is asked.

When relating to a physical or emotional problem, we can use Louise Haye's tables in her books, "You Can Heal Your Body," or "You Can Heal Your Life," since she uses a description of patterns that speak to most people.

For me, pain is something that bothers, disturbs, prevents action, inhibits. For me, the feet symbolize forward motion, progress – movement as opposed to a lack of mobility.

Third stage: **Why am I experiencing this problem at this particular stage of my life?**

Now we will see when and how the problem occurs, and in relation to which situation in our lives. Nothing "just happens," and every problem, emotional or physical, that we experience, is closely linked to the circumstances of our lives. Now we must ask: "When do I experience the problem? When does it crop up? During which period of my life did it occur for the first time?" and so on.

The example I gave – sore feet – occurred every time I had an appointment with a healer in order to work on inhibiting thought patterns... and yet I derived a great deal of pleasure from the appointment, and I was aware of the tremendous change it made in my life.

Now, let's write down the conclusions in a table with four columns:

1. The problem Sore feet

2. The deep subject the problem represents Fear of progress

3. The problem crops up / gets worse when... I want to create a significant change in my life – I am required to assume deep-seated responsibility for my life.

4. Conclusion There is a fear of going forward, of movement, of progress.

* *New thought pattern* I advance with confidence and love, I walk courageously along my physical and spiritual life path, I am happy to take responsibility for my life.

In the last column (*), we will write the new thought pattern we are creating as a substitute for the old thought pattern represented by the subject that is addressed by the problem. Here we actually do "practical" work – exchanging the old subconscious "input" that causes the problem for new healthy and balanced "input" that supports us. However, the very fact of getting to the root of the problem, and even the desire to take responsibility for our lives and understand that we are the ones that cause our problems in order to progress, develop, and understand ourselves and the universe more thoroughly – also make a profound difference in our consciousness.

Thought patterns for creating positive thoughts operate on the subconscious and are very powerful. For that reason, words must be chosen carefully. Positive words must be used, and negative words avoided – such as "I am not afraid of advancing in life," since the subconscious often tends to ignore the word "not" and accepts the sentence without it.

It is important to point out that after working with a table of this type, we begin to think naturally about how thought patterns create emotional and physical realities in our lives. Then the entire process of getting rid of the old input and exchanging it for new input becomes rapid and natural, as does spiritual development.

Now we will move on to the next stage, which is discarding the physical-emotional "clinging" that is linked to the subject of the problem, discardingt the old and bringing in the new. In order to do this, we will prepare a second table with two columns: 1. Positive Thought, and 2. Feeling.

In the first column, we will write the positive thought over and over again. In the parallel column, we will write the feelings the positive thought evokes. These can be emotional or physical. They are the result of the kind of emotion and thought that has sometimes gone on for years – possibly even since childhood. The thought pattern is also active on the cellular layer, and for that reason exerts an influence on the body. Just as we free the thought layer from the unhelpful thought pattern, so we must also free the memories of the emotions and the body. To do that, we have to listen to ourselves carefully, be linked up to ourselves, and detach ourselves from every judgmental thought, so that the feelings can arise by themselves. It is advisable to do this exercise quickly and without thinking so that associations, feelings, and emotions arise naturally.

Positive thought
I advance with confidence and love, I walk courageously along my physical and spiritual life path, I am happy to take responsibility for my life.
Feeling Stomach-ache.

Positive thought I advance with confidence and love, I walk courageously along my physical and spiritual life path, I am happy to take responsibility for my life.
Feeling Unpleasant feeling in the stomach.

Positive thought I advance with confidence and love, I walk courageously along my physical and spiritual life path, I am happy to take responsibility for my life.
Feeling Fear.

Positive thought I advance with confidence and love, I walk courageously along my physical and spiritual life path, I am happy to take responsibility for my life.
Feeling Feeling resembling hunger.

Positive thought I advance with confidence and love, I walk courageously along my physical and spiritual life path, I am happy to take responsibility for my life.

Feeling A little pinch inside

Positive thought I advance with confidence and love, I walk courageously along my physical and spiritual life path, I am happy to take responsibility for my life.

Feeling A memory of a childhood experience of...

Positive thought I advance with confidence and love, I walk courageously along my physical and spiritual life path, I am happy to take responsibility for my life.

Feeling A memory of an experience of...

Positive thought I advance with confidence and love, I walk courageously along my physical and spiritual life path, I am happy to take responsibility for my life.

Feeling Joy

We keep on writing down the positive thought while paying attention to the range of emotional feelings, associations, physical feelings, and memories of experiences and events that arise in us – in short, everything that is evoked in us when we write down the positive thought. We continue until no more unpleasant feelings of any kind arise, and a few more times, until we feel a good and natural feeling about the content of the positive thought, that is, until our subconscious accepts the new thought pattern and adopts it. Of course, the table may well be much longer than the sample one shown above...

When it is a question of a deep and distressing problem,

or when you do not reach a profound insight after the initial practice, you must continue with the table every day for a week. Afterwards, it is advisable to write down the positive thought you created for yourself in a place where you will see it frequently during the day – on the refrigerator, on the bathroom mirror, next to the computer in the study, and so on. Recite the positive thought several times a day. It is not easy to make comprehensive promises in this sphere, but experience has shown time and again that it works. Insights occur, and "problems" give us the gift of their awareness, and after we receive their gift, we no longer need them – so they disappear.

Positive thought and the self-mirror

This exercise is very enjoyable, stimulating, and illuminating. It is very simple, but what it gives us is one of the basic tools for understanding the mode of action of the universe, which tells us over and over again: There is no such thing as "just because," there is nothing that does not have a reason, and there are no encounters and relationships that are insignificant.

We all know someone with whom we do not get along too well, but circumstances dictate that the person is part of our world in some way. This person may be our employer, a colleague, a relative, a friend, or even the friend of a friend.

As we said before, nothing happens "by chance" in the world. We meet various people for various purposes, in the spiritual layer. Some of the encounters constitute repairs of the mind, the soul, or the spirit, and some of them come from interactions in past lives. Some of them serve as a mirror to teach us and be examples of what is still in need of repair and improvement in ourselves, and for increasing our mental and spiritual development. Some of them show the challenges facing us. We have to learn how to surmount the barrier that separates us from the other person. Understanding the "mirror effect" – when the other person in the interaction with us shows us ourselves – is the mind's great understanding of the material world.

A theory that can be put into practice states that it is in our power to change the intensity of the antagonism that occurs in relationships of this type, and this will create an experience that is beneficial and supportive to both sides. It is relatively easy to do. This exercise will be very enlightening for you, and will enable you to discover how positive thought materializes in the physical world. The exercise is performed in two stages. The first occurs during the actual interaction with the person who sparks antagonism or irksome emotions in you, and the second is done at home, with your notebook of spiritual development.

First stage
You are with the person. You make up your mind that today, when you are dealing with him, you are going to think only positive thoughts about him. In your thoughts, tell the person that you know he has a good soul, that he is kind, pleasant, honest – every positive thought you can project to him.

The most important thing is the sincerity of your

intention. You must really believe in these positive thoughts, and this means that you may have to make a bit of an effort to see the person's positive traits. During those moments, at least, there must be no conflict in your beliefs. If you have come across the "mirror effect" in the past, and have assimilated the law of polarity well, you will even be able to send him positive thoughts that are the opposite of his current behavior, because you know that every type of behavior contains the full range of balanced and unbalanced possibilities. For instance, if the person comes through as very egoistic, you can send a loving thought, "You are a wonderful, caring person who supports others." If the person is stingy with love or positive reinforcement (an employer, for example), you can send him the thought, "The love in you is overflowing, you are full of love and permit yourself to show it and share it; you enjoy giving love and making people happy." Perhaps this sounds bombastic and false, but there can never be too much beauty or love. Just avoid "changing" the person or sending him positive thoughts that are somehow linked to you (such as, "You give me positive reinforcement when I do good work"), because they are less effective, and there is something rather manipulative about them. Try to make your thoughts more general; for example, "Your presence and words encourage and support the people around you."

Everyone has good in him, everyone has beauty in him. When we permit ourselves to link up to the channel that enables us to see the person's beauty, we see his beautiful properties on the physical plane as well.

Sometimes, we are so deeply entrenched in anger or hurt that it is not easy to link up to this cosmic channel. In this case, when you cannot find any beautiful property in the person, and it is not easy for you to find the positive pole of his negative behavior, you can send him thoughts such as "I know that deep inside you're good," "The more kindly you behave toward people, the better you'll feel about yourself," "The more you love, the more complete you'll feel." It is well known that many of our behavior problems derive from a lack of self-love (sometimes, from a lack of love for the inner child, who occasionally goes through a small "hell" in his childhood). Therefore, you can send him a thought such as "You love and esteem yourself," "You are learning to love yourself and others," and so on.

However, it is important that you actually believe in your thoughts. For this reason, do not imagine things in which you cannot believe.

The results will surprise you: both the concrete occurrences that occur in front of your eyes in the material world following the projection of positive thoughts – the change in the relationship and in the way the person relates to you (and you to him) – and the inner occurrences of profound insight and spiritual growth to which this line of thinking leads you.

Occasionally, when we begin to project positive thoughts to a particular person, the latter gradually – sometimes even instantaneously – begins to seem different to us, sometimes even physically so. I remember a case in which I met a person who decided to serve as an extremely sharp "mirror" for me (for him, it was a conscious decision, but I didn't know that!). Moreover, he decided to show me the "black holes" that still existed in me. To this end, sitting in my apartment, late at night, after he had actually "forced" me to invite him home, he began to spout forth a lengthy stream of negative thoughts and fears. To start off with, I was astounded. I still didn't know that he was a professional actor who had taken upon himself the meritorious role of showing me what I was afraid of and what I was trying to repress and hide. I experienced a tremendous mass of emotions. Initially, I was angry. "He knows I'm collapsing with exhaustion, and I just want a bit of peace and quiet. What does he want of me?" Then, because of the weird things he was saying, I was frightened. How much hatred and anger there was! I wanted to get away from those energies – I didn't want to accept them. I wanted to shut him up, but I reckoned that his "confession" was important for him, and if I was around, I had to be with him, not against him, for the sake of both of our mental and spiritual processes. Our being together was no coincidence, I thought to myself. I began to send him loving, reinforcing, and supportive thoughts without uttering a word aloud. Suddenly, the same face that had seemed coarse and frightening to me softened and seemed more and more beautiful to me. I began to feel the inner child in him, a hurting, hurt child, a child who had undergone a great deal of suffering that was – incredibly – almost parallel to the suffering my own "inner child" had experienced. When I began to see his inner child crying out for love and self-acceptance, a huge wave of compassion and love swept over me. I felt the same love for myself and for my "inner child" as I felt for the person whose inner child I had taken into my heart. His fears and angers disappeared, and I encouraged him wordlessly and hugged him like a child. After a few moments of a loving hug that was totally compassionate and accepting, he raised his head and looked at me with a smile that was completely different than the frightening expression his face had worn previously, and asked me to always be "me." From that moment on, he behaved totally differently – illuminated and loving. Afterwards I realized that it had been a game (worthy of an Oscar!) whose aim was to have me face the angers, fears, criticism, and judgment toward myself and others that still existed in me.

This little story leads us to the second part of the exercise, in which we will see how the very things that drive us to distraction in other people are in fact a mirror, direct or inverse, of our own behavior. It is a case of "the pot calling the kettle black." This saying contains a profound cosmic truth. Every time a certain type of behavior upsets our mental or emotional equilibrium, it is because there is a link between that property or form of behavior and something in our character. It may be a direct mirror: exactly the same property exists in our character in another variation, and we have not accepted this aspect of our character. It may be an inverse mirror: the person behaves in a way in which we do not permit ourselves to behave because we have convinced ourselves that it is not right, because that's how we were brought up, because the property exists in us in a latent manner and we are afraid of it, and so on. They may be mirrors from the past – mirrors that remind us of events or experiences from our past that we have not yet come to terms with, and still evoke anger, fears, disquiet, and so on. Do the second stage of the exercise in a quiet place. See that you will not be disturbed, and do it when you are completely calm and full of love and self-acceptance.

Second stage

Prepare a table with two or three columns. However, before doing that, you must prepare yourself, since in this exercise you will delve into the essence of the properties that bother you in the other person, and you will find them in yourself in some form. Your starting point will be non-judgment. There is no place for judgment or criticism – not of yourself, and not of the other person. If we were all completely free of shortcomings, we would have nothing to learn or experience in this world. We are in a state of perpetual change, and the "shortcomings" of today are the nucleus of the power of tomorrow, when we understand them. For this reason, the key words for this exercise are *compassion*, *understanding*, and *acceptance* – regarding yourself and the other person.

While you are listing the properties that "irritate" you in the person, remind yourself to try and do this with love. This is very important, since ostensibly this part of the exercise is the opposite of the first stage, because we are listing the person's "shortcomings" and our own. However, everything that is done with understanding, for the sake of learning and spiritual development, is positive – if we refrain from giving vent to the angers that are liable to arise during the attempt to find the "irritating" properties. During the exercise, every time you try to recall the person's "annoying" properties and you experience some kind of unpleasant emotion, say to yourself, "Thank you, I love you," since, as you will see, those properties constitute a direct or inverse mirror of your own properties, or a mirror that reminds you of painful things from the past. In the first column, write down the property that "annoys" you in the person. In the second column, write "Me." In this column, you will see how this property is connected to you, how it appears in you, or if it is lacking in your character. In the third column, write the conclusion and the insight – the reason for the property affecting you and causing your emotional balance to be upset in some way.

I have filled out the table in order to provide an example of how the process can work.

The person's property Speaks about himself a lot.

Me I'm ashamed to speak about myself and praise myself.

Why the property irritates me Inverse mirror – I sometimes want to flatter myself in public, but I'm ashamed to do so.

The person's property Speaks too loudly.

Me Speak softly.

Why the property irritates me As a child, I would speak too loudly, and they always hushed me up. They taught me that it's "forbidden to shout and speak loudly." I'm afraid to make myself heard freely.

The person's property Asks me to do all kinds of things for him.

Me Ask people to do all kinds of things for me.

Why the property irritates me I'm not comfortable with this character trait.

The person's property Speaks obsessively about his love for my friend, speaks about her incessantly whenever we meet.

Me Think obsessively about people I'm in love with, but I'm too shy to share this with others.

Why the property irritates me Jealousy – I'd also like someone to talk about me from morning to night and dream about me like he dreams about my friend.

As we said before, in order for this exercise to be effective, we have to liberate ourselves from judgment and every attempt to justify ourselves. Similarly, we have to be honest with ourselves and fearlessly allow ourselves to expose various traits and imbalances in our character. The idea of the exercise is **discovery**, not criticism or judgment. If you feel a bit confused about the new discoveries you have made about yourself, tell yourself: "Thank you, I love you, I'm progressing and improving more and more each day, I love and value myself at my present standpoint."

Now you certainly see the other person in a different light. You may even thank him for being such an excellent mirror for you, and for contributing to your mental and spiritual development.